The
Therapeutic
Classroom

ERRATUM

The title page should read:

The Therapeutic Classroom

by MONICA HOLMES,
DOUGLAS HOLMES
and JUDITH FIELD

in collaboration with
Arlene Friedman, Janet Geller, M.S.W. and Susan Jaffe

JASON ARONSON, NEW YORK

Monica Holmes

Douglas Holmes

and Judith Field

The
Therapeutic
Classroom

Jason Aronson, New York

Copyright © 1974 by Jason Aronson, Inc.

Library of Congress Cataloging in Publication Data

Holmes, Monica Bychowski.
   The therapeutic classroom

   1. Personnel service in secondary education.
2. Mental hygiene. I. Holmes, Douglas, joint
author. II. Field, Judith, joint author.
III. Title. [DNLM: 1. Adolescent psychiatry.
2. Learning disorders—In adolescence. 3. Milieu
therapy. 4. Remedial teaching. WS462 H752t 1974]
LB1620.5.H64   373.1'4'6   73-81218
ISBN 0-87668-097-X

Designed by Sidney Solomon
Manufactured in the United States of America

This book is dedicated to the memory of my father, Gustav Bychowski, whose early interests as a psychiatrist centered around working with students in a school setting. His death came only two months before the completion of the manuscript, however we often discussed the program and the students which the book describes. His enthusiasm for the work and the ideas presented and his contribution were quite singular.

CONTENTS

Preface

MANY PEOPLE have made this book possible. The program described in the book owes its existence to the Center for Community Research (CCR) of the Associated YM–YWHAs of Greater New York and its commitment to meeting the needs of people. Further, this book has been made possible by CCR's commitment to public communication, rather than to publication in journals that reach only a professional audience. It is for this reason that the Center maintains a writer in residence. Judith Field is a sociologist and writer who turned our ideas, memos, papers, and daily notes on the program into the book that follows.

In the years 1963–1968 I spent five years in the Department of Psychiatry of a large city hospital. In that period I saw little psychotherapy being done that seemed to help the adolescents who came to the clinic. The hospital was designated a Comprehensive Community Mental Health Center, but it was difficult to see how the community was being served.

One small program in child psychiatry did seem to make sense, however. One of my colleagues, with a few psychiatric residents, was providing consultation to a public elementary school. I participated in the workshops for teachers and was impressed with the genuine help given to youngsters in the school by the clinic representatives. Thus, given an opportunity to start a school-based mental health program by the Center for Community Research, I took the chance of creating a mental health unit in the school. This mental health unit began work within a New York City school in 1968. The unit is funded by the New York City Department of Mental Health and Mental Retardation under contract 400019. The program is funded with matching funds provided through the East Flatbush–Rugby YM–YWHA of the Associated YM–YWHAs of Greater New York.

In 1968 the program began as a youth consultation and screening unit. It soon became apparent that screenings were meaningless in the context of long waiting lists for the few existing mental health facilities. What was needed was not screening and referral but actual mental health services. Thus the unit moved out of the Community Center and into the school with the idea of being right in the midst of troubled students. The unit became known as the "Sounding Board." By 1970 it became apparent that this approach had many disadvantages, and the "Academy Model" emerged. This book tells the story of the creation of the Academy and the first year of its existence.

Within the school system we wish to thank the Supervisor of Guidance for the school district in which we worked. He consistently provided support and came to our rescue.

The name of the school and the names of the students have been changed so that their confidences and privacy may be preserved.

Our thanks are extended to the East Flatbush–Rugby YM–YWHA for providing out of school office space for the Sounding Board.

Ida Kagan, the project secretary, has worked with great skill and dedication to maintain the daily process notes and student records. Without her, there would be no Academy record, and this book could not have been written.

Special thanks are due to Linda Melnick, who worked with the Sounding Board as a volunteer for one and a half years with great intelligence and dedication. Her small reading unit actually became the preliminary experience for what later grew into the Academy program.

My greatest thanks go to Arlene Friedman, Janet Geller, and Susan Jaffe. We have worked together for three years in the program and have learned a great deal from each other. The learning, the professional camaraderie, and, of course, the students, have made the experience a memorable one. We are still working on this program, which we hope will be tried by others. I think they will find the work equally exciting and joyous.

Monica Bychowski Holmes Ph.D.
Sounding Board Director

New York City

The
Therapeutic
Classroom

Introduction

THE LEARNING CRISIS among disadvantaged students is nowhere more critical than in early adolescence, when, typically, progress comes to a dead end and problem behavior escalates. Yet the intermediate schools tend to be the most neglected area in public education. One reason for this situation is the unexplored belief, encouraged by highly tentative and undocumented developmental theories, that academic deficits are irreversible after the elementary years. This book offers concrete evidence to the contrary and concrete arguments as to why.

The evidence stems from a front-line effort to reverse the psychological and academic disabilities of young adolescents who were the rejects of a big city public school. In simplest terms, its takeoff point is the recognized interdependence between learning and emotional dynamics. Few educational innovations could have been conducted under less promising circumstances. An *ad hoc* undertaking, it was launched in haste without adequate preliminaries. It took place under completely realistic conditions, in what could be characterized most optimistically as a skeptical school environment. It was a trial-and-error operation, guided by no pretested blueprint but by an untried perspective, a venture into uncharted waters. This *ad hoc* nature is to be emphasized, as it underlines the significance of a breakthrough that occurred despite a host of countervailing factors.

There are practical reasons for writing this book. No adequate model or curriculum exists for our target group. As a matter of fact, many educators feel that no model can be developed for the vast student population past early childhood that is unable to learn and that, year after year, moves out of the schools lacking the skills and knowledge necessary for effective functioning. The therapeutic classroom, with its fusion of teaching and therapy, provides the basis for such a model. In its initial trial the fusion produced results that neither therapy nor pedagogy seem able to achieve by themselves. Beyond the specific methods and strategies employed, the results can be traced to a concept that opens up a new world of possibilities for dealing with learning failure.

There is a famous optical illusion in which a picture is ambiguous: It can be perceived either as a symmetrical vase or as two human profiles facing each other. The physical object is the same, but the phenomenon perceived varies dramatically. The therapeutic classroom concept also involves a dramatic perceptual shift. The idea for a new kind of classroom with mental health techniques incorporated directly into everyday operations stems from an altered way of looking at the epidemic problem of academic failure and disruptive behavior. It represents a fundamental redefinition of the problem arising from this changed perception, which makes new remedies available. There is, after all, nothing surprising about this change. The definition of a problem will determine the means used for its solution. Thus, when efforts at solution consistently fail, it would seem reasonable to suspect the definitions from which they have proceeded.

In our case, the perceptual shift entailed was a recognition of the inseparable mutual cause-and-effect relationship between learning difficulties and emotional disabilities, particularly during early adolescence. In the light of this perception, it is not fruitful to regard and to deal with each problem as a separate entity; there are, in fact, not two problems but only one. It can only be dealt with as a whole. It also follows that, in the intermediate school, the usual neat division of labor by professional category, of learning to the classroom and personal adjustment to the clinic, is an exercise in futility. One way or another, for significant gains to occur, a merger of therapy and teaching must take place in an ongoing collaboration geared to realistic needs.

Such a break from traditional professional thought calls for some explanation. In this case it has a history going back to the decision of a mental health unit to try a new procedure for reaching young adolescents. The difficulties of working with this age group are well known and widespread. In an attempt to bypass the difficulties, the Center for Community Research took the step of offering its services in a flexible, informal format directly within a junior high school, instead of at an outside location. With this first move off the beaten path, accumulating experience made forcefully apparent what could only be conjectured in the isolation of the classical clinic setting. This was the extent to which school failure and destructive psychological patterns are tied together and the extent to which a disorienting school structure contributes to both.

5

The therapeutic classroom experiment, imperfect as it was, presents dramatic evidence of what can happen when learning failure and emotional disabilities are treated as one indivisible problem. Even more importantly, it showed that adolescents who cannot function in the public schools do not have to be abandoned as another lost generation. True enough, in the long run, the most effective antidote to the failure that is epidemic in our schools, especially among minority and disadvantaged students, is not prophylaxis but prevention.

It would be best to eliminate the malady through early childhood intervention, correcting deficits before they become cumulative. For hundreds of thousands of children, however, it is too late for the sensible long-range view. At the age of twelve and thirteen they are already the casualties of an educational and social system that they never made and moving into adolescence branded as terminal cases. The stakes are much too high to accept this prognosis. This book is being written to show that it doesn't have to be that way.

CHAPTER 1

Profiles in Failure

*A*NYONE FAMILIAR with those we term the "losers" in our urban junior high schools will recognize the Academy students. Angry, apathetic, disruptive, defensive—their behavior involves a desperate attempt to maintain a core of self-respect in the face of chronic failure. Sometimes this attempt takes the form of aggressive behavior; sometimes it shows up as hostile immobility; sometimes it appears as truancy, a retreat from a painful reality. Many of these children are virtually incapable of self-control. They are mistrustful, anxious, incapable of being friends with adults, unable to tolerate frustration.

Most are from economically and socially impoverished   7

backgrounds that, coupled with ethnic and racial minority status, lend fuel to the fire in a mixed school like Kennedy Junior High. This school has a student population of 1,200 that in 1970 was over 50 percent white and middle class.

Academy students—the focus of this book—were behavior problems well known to the authorities for fighting, cutting, truancy, and disruptive behavior in general. Four of them had been suspended, two of them more than once. Thirty-two of the thirty-seven had been reported for truancy the year before, twenty-five (or two-thirds) ten times or more, and five of them fifty times or more. All except four had been reported for disruptive behavior, and fifteen had been specifically reported for fighting.

Problem behavior, however, was not the basis on which they had been recruited for the program. For an explanation of selection and recruitment it is necessary to go back to the genesis of the program and anticipate somewhat the full account that appears in Chapter 4.

The idea of setting up special classes for low-achieving ninth graders had started out as something quite different from what finally emerged as the Academy program. In an effort to counteract mounting tensions, the school had secured funds for a work–study project, with students to attend classes in the morning and leave for jobs in the afternoon. Neither a remedial nor a therapeutic component had been included or considered. Students had already been selected, simply on the basis of whether or not they wanted to work for half a day, and four teachers had been assigned to them.

It was at this point that we asked the school to let us convert the two work–study groups into therapeutic classes. For a year and a half we had been working in the school as a mental health unit operating on a model of one-to-one clinical service. We called ourselves the "Sounding Board" and had an office in the school building staffed with a full-time social worker, two graduate students in clinical psychology, who each came two days a week, and a supervising clinical psychologist one day a week. Increasingly, our experience had brought home to us the need for a different approach with the failures, disrupters, and truants who are unable to articulate their problems and are not reached by the techniques of conventional insight therapy. Now we would try a wholly new model. What it called for was a radical restructuring of the school environment for those young adolescents who need the input of mental health techniques in order to start learning.

We set up three requirements for the students who would come into the therapeutic classes. They were to be of "average" intelligence, have no overt organic impairment, and be at least three years below grade level in reading. Guided by these criteria, we sifted through the roster of the work–study classes, selecting those whose reading scores conformed to our limit. There followed interviews and tests with each of these youngsters.

At the end of the selection and screening process we had, in a few busy weeks, recruited thirty-seven ninth-grade students, the majority of whom read at or below the fifth-grade level and were unable to do simple arithmetic. Yet they all showed "average" intellectual potential as indicated by their scores on certain subtests of the Wechsler Intelligence Test for Children.* All had agreed to participate in a program that would help them catch up in reading and math.

These were thirty-seven different individuals. However, common patterns and similar personality dynamics were operating among them. Building on elements shown by most, a description of where six "typical" students were during the first weeks of the academy follows.

* The three subtests were Similarities, Block Design, and Vocabulary.

Kenneth

Some adolescents become behavior problems because they have difficulty maintaining control. Not Kenneth. He was very much in control and very sure of who he was. When he ignored orders or threw insolent challenges at adults, he knew exactly what he was doing. He was showing them that he was as good as they, and if they didn't like it, that was too bad. They didn't care what *he* liked, so you could say that he was simply returning the compliment.

If the Academy were merely a program to deal with troublemakers, Kenneth would have been a leading candidate. He was known throughout the school as someone to watch out for, by both teachers and by students. He was said to have extorted money from others in the school, and one story had it that he threatened to beat up a teacher after class. The story may not have been true, but everyone believed that it was. He was a big, powerfully built boy with dark skin and a belligerent slouch who looked tough and talked tough. Even more intimidating than his verbal threats was the menacing way he had of staring at people. Even before Kenneth opened his mouth, teachers would be on guard.

They had been on guard against him even before he came into the school. Kenneth had been preceded by several brothers, all of whom had become known as serious discipline problems, and his role of public enemy was tailor-made and waiting for him when he arrived at Kennedy. It must be said, however, that he showed little reluctance to take it on. One of the principal ways in which he did so was to get into power struggles with anyone in a position of authority. He was, it seemed, carrying on a running one-man war against the system, against "them."

10

Until the Academy program got organized, we only knew about Kenneth because of his reputation. This was not the kind of adolescent who was likely to bring himself or his problems to a social worker or, indeed, to feel that he had any problems to bring. The first actual contact any of us had with him was during the screening interviews in the late spring. He was among those in the original group who had volunteered for a work–study class in order to get a job. We explained to him, as to the others, that the purpose of the class had changed to include improving reading skills, although he would still be able to work in the afternoon, and that was fine with him. He could see that improving his skills would be a good idea.

All in all, there was nothing at this interview to indicate that the boy we were talking to was one of the school's chief troublemakers. He seemed perfectly reasonable and responsive. It was at this point that we did learn a few things about him we had not known before. We found out that he had always been in one of the lowest-level classes and that he rarely, if ever, had paid attention in class or done any work. He just didn't find it interesting. What he did find interesting was playing basketball. He was good at it, but the coach would not take him on the team, because his marks were too poor.

Kenneth's behavior in class as school began scarcely came as a surprise. It was exactly what we had been led to expect—the defiance, challenge, hostility. There were a few developments, however, that did not seem to fit the picture. For one thing, Kenneth was making a lot of positive contributions to discussions about what the class was doing and how it should be conducted. It was noteworthy that when he did the other students listened to him with marked respect. So did the staff. What he said showed considerable maturity and intelligence.

11

Frank

According to the daily report, the following incident occurred on the first day of school in Academy B. "One of the boys got very excited about the room being too hot and wanted the windows opened from the bottom. He practically blew up when the teacher insisted it was against the rules and, finally, walked over and opened them himself. This looks like one boy whose frustration tolerance is just about nil." That was Frank. He was hardly one of the self-effacing ones. You could not easily overlook the fact that he was there—arguing, challenging, complaining, losing his self-control over a minor provocation.

Frank's low frustration level had marked and marred his school career, making it impossible for him to do any consistent work and getting him into constant difficulties with teachers and students. He was a poor student, and he should not have been, because he had the ability to do well. But he couldn't use this ability. Give Frank an assignment and, at the first hint of a problem, he was ready to give up, which usually meant an angry explosion. Typically, he would spit out an appropriate curse word in Italian and tear apart what he was doing. He had also been known to grab the books or equipment he was working with and hurl them across the room, a fairly serious matter when laboratory or shop materials were involved.

Any time that things went wrong, Frank would lash out at whatever or whomever seemed to be frustrating him. Consequently, he was high on the list of the school's discipline problems. Teachers kept reporting him to the dean's office for his outbursts in class. In the previous year he had been suspended twice for fighting in school. He was a fairly slim, unathletic boy, but that didn't stop him from taking on anyone who stepped on his toes. It was characteristic of Frank that the fights he got into were unpremedi-

12

tated affairs that took place under the nose of the authorities.

Of course, he hated school and would, he insisted in the screening interview, have liked nothing better than to drop out and go to work. The only reason he was still there was that his mother said he had to go. He and his friends only wanted to be in the program so they could leave in the afternoons. There were three of them who were buddies. They were all volatile, aggressive teenagers from working-class Italian homes, very conscious of their manhood and the need to show how tough they were and unanimously scornful of anything to be gained from books.

In the first few weeks of school, as the classes got into many open discussions and exchanges—something none of them had experienced before—Frank quickly became one of the most conspicuous members of Academy B. Whatever the subject up for discussion—whether it was rules for latecomers, the pros and cons of breaking up into small groups, or how everyone felt about being in this kind of class—there was Frank dominating the scene with a loud, steamroller voice that drowned out everyone else. Everything was lousy and everyone was stupid was the gist of what he had to say. The impression he left was of a figure jumping up and down with a great big open mouth. It was hardly the picture of a boy with any active or potential concern for the feelings of others.

Doris

We called it doing a "war dance," and Doris Perez was an expert at it, although she was not the only one. What it involved was getting started on a grievance or an act of defiance and then becoming more and more worked up to the point of hysteria. With Doris nothing seemed to help once she got going, an angry, punitive reaction least of all.

13

That had been tried by every teacher she had ever had, as well as her guidance counselors, grade advisors, and the disciplinary deans. Doris' fury seemed to escalate with threats and punishment.

Conventional therapy in her case had made no contribution toward resolving the problem. The previous year, Doris had been one of our most regular and least successful clients. Although she seemed eager enough to come for appointments and to talk over what was on her mind, her treatment really got nowhere in producing any constructive understanding or inner controls. The difficulty seemed to be that Doris became so involved with any problem she discussed that it was impossible to reach her. Having her join the Academy classes represented another attempt at reaching her through the entirely different approach of improving her reading and math skills, which were very weak. She was all for that and for the informal idea of the class when we talked to her about it in June.

In September, however, Doris had changed—vehemently! She did *not* want to be in the class, she did not belong in the class, and she was *not* going to be in it. This was a class for "dummies" and for "crazies," and she wasn't either one. To emphasize the point she refused to participate, but her withdrawal was not passive. For example, she and two of her friends engaged in loud and animated conversations in Spanish, complete with giggling and significant looks at other people whom, it was to be understood, they were discussing. More often she expressed herself more actively and conspicuously. She would run in and out of the room, bang on cabinets, lock herself in the closet, yell and scream at the top of her lungs—sometimes in high spirits and sometimes in fury.

Instead of subsiding as the weeks went on, her angry tactics intensified. Increasingly she appeared to be directing her hostility at the Sounding Board staff. It started to become a regular routine for her to whisper disparaging remarks about what we were wearing loudly enough to set the whole class laughing. Then she began to go further calling out remarks like "Why are you wearing those shoes?" or "Why don't you comb your hair?" If one of us were involved with her group, she would create an uproar, making violent objections to what we were doing. On several occasions she ran out of the classroom. When we locked the door to prevent her getting back in, she stood outside pounding on it furiously.

Why was she acting this way? What made her so unreachable? All that she seemed to be accomplishing by these actions was to get a lot of attention.

Martin

It tells a great deal about Martin that there was no mention of him in the daily reports of the Academy classes until several weeks of the term had gone by. He was the good boy, the one who goes unnoticed. In the process of not noticing him, one also fails to observe that he is not doing and cannot do any of the work the class is involved in.

"Martin? He must be that nice blond boy who always sits by himself in the back of the room."

That's the way it was with Martin at the beginning of the year. The class was still organized as a single unit most of the time. Martin would sit in a back corner of the room, silent, bothering no one, going through the motions of following what was going on. No one really knew that he was there. It is a sure-fire system for getting by for someone who feels stupid and ashamed of it. No teacher is going to bother him, if he just minds his own business. They have their hands full with the troublemakers. The system had been working for Martin for many years now.

That it worked in the Academy for the first few weeks was partly the result of an accident that kept us from realizing what Martin was up to. As it happened, he was one of the two students in the Academy who had not been tested or interviewed in advance. He failed to show up for his appointment, and during the hectic preparation period in the late spring we had no time to track him down. Later it became apparent that missing the appointment was no accident; it was part of a consistent technique for avoiding exposure.

Then, however, we did not worry about it particularly. He had been okayed for the career guidance project, was already working at a job in a hobby shop, and had nothing in his record to indicate a problem. While his reading score was extremely low—barely third grade—he was not the only one at that level. He was assigned to Academy A with the poorer readers who were also, most of them, in the bottom ability range on the WISC subtests.

It is interesting that one of the first references to Martin in the daily reports—three weeks after the term started—is a surprised reaction to his high level of comprehension during a science lesson given to a group of five boys. The comment reads: "I came away with a great deal of respect for his innate intelligence and general ability. It seems clear to me that this is a student who is being unchallenged and some-how underutilized." No one on the staff had realized this about Martin before.

Nor had we had the chance to realize something else. This boy of fifteen could, in fact, hardly read at all. As we moved to a small-group operation and he was forced to participate with the others in reading aloud, it became obvious that his inability to read was terribly painful to him. The maneuvers he engaged in to avoid detection during this first period of exposure bore the marks of desperation. He fidgeted, walked around, asked for a bathroom pass, sat himself in a chair where he would be the last one called on, or simply refused to try.

Still, at this point, there seemed no reason why Martin should not improve tremendously once he started to put in hard, concentrated work with a slow-moving remedial group. We had, however, failed to reckon on several crucial elements in the situation. One of these involved his behavior pattern, for now that he was unable to hide, the "good" boy started to become disruptive.

Barbara

She was a pretty and smart-looking girl with lovely copper skin and a well-groomed Afro who carried herself with an air of self-assurance. Talking to friends, Barbara was confident, open, animated, very much in charge of the situation. With teachers or other adults in authority—white adults, that is—things became different. Then her face turned into a sullen mask, her speech into a series of sarcastic monosyllables, and her entire manner simmered with defiance. In class she had a simple and effective technique for expressing this attitude. She played deaf. What do you do with a student who insists, "I didn't hear you?" Most teachers found her too difficult and left her alone, which seemed to be what she wanted.

The decision to take Barbara into the Academy program was a calculated risk, because of her record for fighting. "You'll be sorry," school authorities warned us. Last year in the eighth grade Barbara had been a ringleader in the fighting that went on among the girls, and she was considered incorrigible. Her hostility toward the white adult world was something we were prepared to tackle, but we could not afford to have the project jeopardized by someone who created serious trouble. In her screening interview we brought up the matter without hedging. Yes, she said, she had been in a lot of fights, but she didn't want to behave that way any more. She spoke with such apparent honesty that we decided to take a chance.

The reason we did was that she seemed eager to be in the program. Unlike most of the other Academy students she had sought us out. Now that she was almost ready for high school, Barbara said, she wanted to become a better student. She had heard that we were really going to help students improve their reading and math. From some of her remarks it did occur to us that a good deal of this interest may have been her mother's rather than her own. Still, even with pressure from home, not many young adolescents will take the initiative as she had.

As the program got under way, we began to have doubts. Barbara's hostility went much deeper than we had realized. She was openly antagonistic to the group discussions and refused to take part in them. "That's not any of your business," she snapped when asked to tell how she felt about being in the class. What concerned us even more was that she had quickly drawn to her and dominated several other black girls who appeared ready to follow her lead.

Despite all the previous declarations about improving her skills, Barbara was also resisting the work and complaining that it was "babyish." She would sit to the side with subtraction problems in front of her and seem busy working on them. If one of us came up to her, though, she would cover the paper, take out her make-up, and begin putting it on with great concentration. Sometimes, when she saw us approach, she would quickly take out a magazine.

At first, we thought that Barbara's behavior sprang out of anger and a deep lack of trust. Little by little, as we grew to know her better, we began to wonder if something else might be involved.

Richard

Here was a good-natured, black, fifteen-year-old, whom everyone wanted to help but with whom no one and nothing had succeeded, including an entire year of individual therapy with the Sounding Board. To help Richard it would first be necessary to have him stop his disruptive behavior and to do at least a little academic work. As it was, he had acquired and maintained one of the school's poorer academic and worst discipline records.

The complaints in his thick file took in not only disorderliness and truancy but fighting and vandalism. They had brought him several suspensions, a court appearance, and very nearly expulsion from school. Only by the grace of overcrowding in the city's institutions for problem students was Richard available to the Academy. Nevertheless, for all the seriousness of his situation, most of Richard's misbehavior could hardly be described as anything more than fooling around. The fact that there was so much of this behavior made him a problem in school.

His primary form of misbehavior during his first two years in Kennedy Junior High was to roam the halls "illegally" or to disrupt his classes by clowning. With someone like Richard in the classroom it was impossible to teach. He would, for instance, giggle without restraint, talk incessantly, tell uproarious jokes to his neighbors, comb his hair ostentatiously, create chaos by playfully hitting a pal on the head. When a teacher insisted that he stop, Richard would then pick himself up and walk out. That's the way he acted when he was in school. Very often, however, he simply was not there. He did not come, or if he did come, he would arrive late and cut class afterwards.

On one occasion Richard's clowning had gone too far. Fooling around with some cronies on a bus, he had succeeded in breaking a window and had been summoned to juvenile court. It was then that he came to the Sounding Board office for help. Because he came on his own, it seemed to us that he might be open to insight. We could not have been more mistaken. We spent the year trying to work out with him why he acted the way he did and got nowhere. Yes, he was bothered about getting a court record, but, outside of that, nothing really mattered. Did he want to get thrown out of school? He didn't care. Wouldn't he like to do better in his studies? What for? He had no motivation to change, and we finally had to admit defeat. We were unable to reach him in a traditional manner.

It was with misgivings that we decided to take Richard into the Academy. A boy who was that unreachable could jeopardize the whole project. Why did we take the chance? Because his test scores showed an average learning potential despite his poor achievement, because there seemed nothing pathological in his personality dynamics, and because, frankly, we had already invested so much in him. Besides, we liked him.

For the first few weeks we were not sure that we had made the right decision. Richard carried on in the Academy exactly as he always had before. He fooled around, created disorder, came in late, refused to work. He had been placed in the lower-achieving of our two classes, and even there he was among the poorest students. It wasn't until a little time had passed that we realized how minimal his skills were.

CHAPTER 2

The New Consequences of Failure

A DANGEROUS GAME of make-believe is being played with the children of the poor. It is going on in public schools and mental health clinics throughout the country. The "game" is particularly dangerous for adolescents, who are uniquely vulnerable. It involves the pretense that learning is taking place, or that therapy is taking place, when all evidence shouts to the contrary. In fact, what is taking place is the performance of professional rituals followed by tragic consequences. The operations may be successful, but the patients are dying.

In the area of mental health the waste of time, money, and expertise is tremendous. Adolescents from disadvantaged populations constitute a high-risk group, particularly vulnerable to emotional disorders related to the hard facts of poverty, discrimination, and educational failure. Their need for therapeutic help has been described as "desperate." Yet mental health agencies persist in a system of service delivery that is irrelevant to both their needs and their lifestyle and that, therefore, is largely ineffective.

Observing one of these mental health clinics in operation is like watching an updated version of *Don Quixote*. Instead of tilting their lances at imaginary villains, psychotherapists are earnestly engaged in treating imaginary patients. At weekly case conferences, which are models of professional protocol, skilled psychiatrists and psychologists can be heard developing diagnoses and prescribing treatments that disregard the stresses, values, and attributes common to lower-class life. Prescription for treatment rarely departs from the convention of once-a-week psychotherapy, the traditional fifty-minute hour geared to the development of insight through the medium of language.

With the middle-class population that was the source and fountainhead of this approach, such an approach may, and often does, work well. With low-income groups it is transparently inadequate. For example, the explanatory theories fail to explain because of their specialized frame of reference. A classic demonstration occurred when a well-known child analyst visited one of the municipal mental health clinics in a big city. He had agreed to conduct a psychotherapeutic session in front of a one-way screen, a rare opportunity for the staff to observe a master in action. The event never came about, however, because the "right" patient could not be found. Among the hundreds of children seen by the agency, there was not one whose problems fitted the famous doctor's influential model.

Equally unrealistic for disadvantaged adolescents is the treatment formula of once-a-week psychotherapy. Adolescents from low-income families are notoriously unreliable as clinic patients; in many instances they simply refuse to come after an initial visit, typically made under coercion. When they do keep appointments, very little of a therapeutic nature takes place. Typically, they have been referred by the school for acting-out behavior and strongly resist the notion that they have a problem to talk about or that talking about problems makes any sense. They are defensive and hypersensitive about going to the "shrink," which implies that they are "crazy." They are hostile to adults and resent having to tell a total stranger what they are feeling. In sum, a working relationship is almost never established with low-income adolescents in a clinic setting.

Mental health professionals are neither fools nor charlatans. They are well aware that something is wrong, just as school professionals recognize that something is seriously wrong with education as it involves minorities and low-income groups. Unfortunately, in both professions the overwhelming tendency is to see the fault as lying in the client rather than in the service delivery. If only the children of the poor were different, there would be no problem! From this viewpoint the logical remedy is to change the children, a feat that must be undertaken at an early age before the ravages of deprivation become irreversible. As Larner (1968) has put it: "But what difference does high school make? The battle is lost by the time 1st graders move to the 2nd grade, when only 10 percent of them are at reading level" (p. 136).

In the meanwhile, the pretense of education continues. As the situation stands now, the secondary schools which disadvantaged adolescents are legally obliged to attend may look like institutions of learning, but the resemblance is largely coincidental. Literally millions of frustrated and rebellious youngsters play out a waiting game in them, going through a succession of meaningless rituals. In a report to

23

the New York City Board of Education early in 1972, for instance, Bard (1972) made the following points about the city's high schools:

A primary cause of failure in these schools is reading retardation. Yet the schools place students years behind in reading into regular literature and social studies courses where they are totally lost.

As many as 80 percent of the students fail algebra in some city high schools. They have never learned elementary arithmetic and do not read well enough to understand the problems.

Teachers address disadvantaged students in terms which are incomprehensible to them. Lessons are conducted and questions posed in a fashion which presupposes resources of information the students have never acquired (p. 78).

Such indictments of the public schools serving disadvantaged adolescents have become commonplace. Among concerned observers there is a singular unanimity about the continuing failure of urban schools to meet the educational needs of lower-income students, especially at the secondary level. To quote Shanker (1972): "Almost all the students who enter junior high schools without knowing how to read, write and compute graduate from such schools without having learned these essential skills. By the time the students reach a certain age, schools as now organized do not seem to make any significant contribution to the learning process" (p. 5).

Reiterating the theme, the report of a recent study of seven hundred high schools in forty five cities with populations above 300,000 asserts that "the big cities of the country are in deep trouble educationally speaking" (Hechinger, 1970). In the inner core of the larger cities, it was found, as many as 25 or 30 percent of all sixteen and seventeen-year-olds fail to learn and later fail to get jobs or make satisfactory adult adjustments. Significantly, the authors report these schools to be remarkably similar in terms of curriculum and approach. They are rigidly anchored in a system developed for a different population and different times. Commenting on these findings, the education editor of the *New York Times* wrote: "The prescription for the sick big-city schools is clearly to throw away the mold and develop new patterns" (Hechinger, 1970).

Whatever the underlying factors generating school failure, the immediate handicap that bars disadvantaged youngsters from genuine learning is their lack of reading and language skills. Why poor kids make poor readers is a mystery that continues to baffle the best-intentioned experts. Looking for a reasonable explanation, one finds a wide choice of hotly debated and contradictory views, ranging from cultural deprivation in the home to colonial oppression in the classroom. The straight, external facts, however, are beyond debate. In the schools as they are now constituted, despite all so-called "compensatory" efforts, children from low-income populations fall behind in reading almost as soon as their formal schooling begins. Furthermore, as they move through the grades, these children fall further and further behind.

Far from improving, the situation seems to be worsening. According to Clark (1970), there is strong evidence to suggest that the average academic achievement of minority group students has been regressing from year to year in the urban public schools. In New York City 1971 reading tests, taking a further drop from the preceding year, showed two-thirds of all elementary and junior high school pupils below the national norm for their grades. Following the pattern of a cumulative deficit, the gap widened from two months below standard as the median score in the second grade to a year and eight months behind the national norm in grade seven (Buder, 1972b, p. 55).

The extent to which reading disabilities are tied to poverty status stands out dramatically in these New York City test results, which showed a steadily increasing disparity between pupils in middle-income areas and those attending schools in depressed neighborhoods. In the higher grades the disparity became mammoth. The eighth-grade median score at a middle-class junior high school was two years *above* the national norm. The four junior high schools in a ghetto area were all three years or more *behind* the norm and *five years or more behind the middle-class school* (Buder, 1972b, p. 55).

The same situation can be documented wherever school populations include large numbers of lower-class children, whatever their racial or ethnic backgrounds.

That the factor of race does indeed compound the handicaps of poverty is undeniable. It does so in a variety of overt and covert ways: by aggravating teachers' negative expectations, heightening the demoralizing effects of segregated education, diminishing motivation as a response to the realistic fact of prejudice and discrimination. A wealth of evidence shows, however, that the roots of school failure are not racial but socioeconomic. For example, in a recent report on public education in Duluth, Minnesota, Hubert (1972), describes the kind of student apathy and lack of achievement that have come to be associated with ghetto schools There is a lack of excitement in the faces of the children, he reports, and a look of despair. "By fourth grade, there's talk of dropping out of school as soon as possible, of fights and drunken brawls among parents and parents' friends, and of not having had breakfast" (p. 57). The schools that these children attend rank far below the national median on standardized achievement tests despite generous expenditures. They may sound like ghetto schools but are far from it with respect to racial composition. The city of Duluth is 97 percent white, and these are schools with a high proportion of children from low-income white families.

26   Weintraub (1972), reporting on a long-term survey that

followed 17,000 children from birth, presents an even bleaker picture, again reminiscent of ghetto conditions in the United States. The results found working-class children at an early age showing hostility towards teachers, withdrawal, depression, and a writing off of adult standards. The average gap in reading attainment between the least advantaged and the most advantaged was over four years. Another description of minority schools in an American city? Not at all. These research findings are from a study of British children published in the spring of 1972. They are consistent with the data from many other investigations in Great Britain since the end of World War II, when a serious effort to democratize the British educational system got under way.

In the United States in 1941 and 1942 a now-famous study focusing on social class and adolescent behavior was conducted in a small midwestern town. Findings revealed the devastating impact of low social class position on achievement in high school. Among other things, lower-class youngsters had a much higher percentage of failures, scored lower on intelligence tests, and dropped out of school at an earlier age. Of the high school age group in town, almost 90 percent from the lowest class had left school, while all of the youngsters in the two highest social classes were in attendance. Rich and poor, these were all white children in a population that was 93 percent native-born (Hollingshead, 1949).

There is a reasonable objection that might be raised to this evidence. Why is it, one might ask, that the public schools in this country worked so well in the past, with preceding generations of the poor? What is different now that the system that was once one of our most vaunted institutions is now failing? According to an increasing consensus among authorities, the answer is painfully simple. The system never worked. The sentimental picture in the history textbooks of American public education providing

27

the major avenue of access into American society for the children of the poor is mythology. There has always been, Katz (1971), declares, "a pathetic lack of fit between the poor and the schools" (p. 139). Brenton (1970), points out: "Many of the children of the poor have always fallen by the wayside educationally" (p. 173). However, the numbers are now greater, and the social consequences potentially more devastating.

There is nothing new about the game of make-believe in the public schools, nor about the factors responsible for it. A recent study argues that the die was cast by about 1880, when American education acquired a bureaucratic, class-biased structure that has not altered fundamentally since that time. The result has been school systems that throughout have separated children along class lines. Katz (1971) states: "There is a great gap between the pronouncement that education serves the people and the reality of what schools do to and for the children of the poor. Despite the existence of free, universal and compulsory schooling, most poor children become poor adults" (p. xviii). He terms the belief that schools in the past provided a solid training in basic skills and opened up avenues of social mobility a "regressive fantasy".

The failure of the public schools with disadvantaged students is not new, but its consequences are. Where once the dropouts and undereducated could find a self-respecting, if lowly, place in American society, now the only place for them is on the outside. As recently as two decades ago people with little schooling were able to gain entry into the economic system in a variety of occupations that required little more than a "strong back and a weak mind," to quote a time-honored American expression. A lucky few could even work their way into comparative affluence. But the situation has changed radically. With accelerating advances in automation and technology, the occupational structure of the United States has undergone a swift and revolutionary alteration. More and more of the unskilled jobs in agriculture, mining, construction, and manufacturing once available to the undereducated have been eliminated. The technological revolution in agriculture alone displaced approximately twenty million Americans from the land between 1940 and 1970 and is largely responsible for the huge migration of the poor into urban areas (Piven and Cloward, 1971).

The failure of the schools in the present era culminates in a life sentence of deprivation for the youngsters who are semiliterate when they drop out or, indeed, even when they graduate from high school. Such preordained futures already number in the millions, with each year adding almost a million more, calculating on the basis of dropouts alone (Maeroff, 1972). But the problem is not confined to dropouts. A high school diploma in itself by no means provides a passport to creditable employment. Too many are little more than palliatives given to young people who, in fact, lack the basic reading, writing, and computing skills that are minimal qualifications for productive work in today's economy. Without these skills, diploma or not, there is nowhere to go for a livelihood but intermittent menial employment or the welfare office. Without them an individual is relegated to the status of a second-class citizen unable to cope with job applications, tax forms, or the daily newspaper.

How many second-class citizens can this country afford? If the consequences of school failure have new implications for the individual victims, they also pose an unprecedented threat to the entire society. On the one hand, an ever-increasing army of unwanted young people with no future in the system is "social dynamite," especially in a society that promises equality and opportunity to all and visibly produces it for the majority. The explosive possibilities have already surfaced in violent school disorders, riots, and

29

criminal activities. Not long ago it was charged that more than 60,000 of the 200,000 New York City pupils who are absent daily from school are truants who wander the streets engaging in antisocial behavior that menaces the citizenry (Buder, 1972a). On the other hand, at a more fundamental level there will soon be an estimated twenty million Americans dependent for their support on welfare making up a caste of pariahs whose desperate circumstances, say the experts, are linked "beyond dispute" with inadequate education (Venn, 1970).

At this point we should make our own position clear. When we started to work with adolescents in a public school, our efforts were addressed to mental health problems. As mental health professionals, we were disturbed by the irrelevance and ineffectiveness of therapeutic efforts directed at troubled adolescents from disadvantaged population. We ourselves had taken part in programs operating with the conventional, clinical approaches and had been shaken by the futility of these efforts and the tremendous needs going unmet.

We knew that the public schools were also meeting with failure, that the consequences were grave, and that many proposals for remedy were being advanced. Not until we were working within the confines of a public school and saw the traditional educational system in action did we grasp the extent of its tragic inadequacy in relation to the disadvantaged youngsters who were its failures and its rejects. It was then that we discovered—we could hardly avoid doing so—the uniquely destructive role of the junior high school framework in cutting off the prospect for progress at this critical age. To our dismay we also learned that while there is no dearth of solutions being sought for remedying the learning deficits that plague the poor, pitifully few are directed past the elementary level.

Concern about the learning failure of children from disadvantaged backgrounds and the outpouring of resources into remedial efforts has concentrated on the early years largely as the result of recent research and theory in child development. Cognitive psychologists have produced powerful evidence and arguments regarding the importance of ages one to seven years for the development of intelligence. This emphasis has led to the neglect of the older child. What has not been sufficiently emphasized is the tentative and speculative nature of the prevailing cognitive theory, which often rests more on provocative hypotheses than on scientific proof, about the all-determining impact of early stimulation. This is not to argue against the promising possibilities of early childhood programs and remedial innovation in the elementary years; it is to argue against the foreclosure of hope for the child who has reached adolescence.

We are writing off millions of young people and justifying it in the name of the current fashion in behavioral science. Mayer has put the issue well: "The argument for greatly enriched pre-school experience is certainly strong enough without an insistence on eternal damnation for those not lucky enough to enjoy it" (Miller, 1967, p. 42). Miller (1967) has pointed up the dangers of exclusive emphasis on the young child, calling it an "ideology,":

I fear that we are beginning to move toward the possibility of a do-nothing policy in regard to making sweeping changes in the school. For example, the present emphasis upon pre-kindergarten education as basically necessary for the advance of low-income kids is terribly exaggerated.

. . . . Increasingly the notion is being spread that if kids cannot make school by grade one or by grade three, they can have no educational future. The school does not really have to bother to try to do something in the later years, because the essential emphasis is upon the child's ability to succeed early (p. 42).

In the meanwhile, as we discovered at Kennedy Junior High, the children who enter the seventh grade with a learning deficit can anticipate very little but custodial care and increasing feelings of inadequacy and inferiority. By the time they leave junior high school at the end of the ninth grade, they will be practically at the same place where they started academically, but far more damaged psychologically by a now-indelible stigma of failure. In the process many of them will also have settled down into a career of disruptive behavior that is one kind of self-protective response to the punishing situation in which they find themselves trapped.

A reading survey carried out by the school in 1970 documented the pattern of failure. In a school of approximately 1,300 children, half were reading below grade level and one-quarter were two years behind. More disheartening, students in the least advanced classes, which constituted 50 percent of the student population, improved less than one grade level in reading throughout their entire three-year tenure at Kennedy Junior High. The median grade level of those in the nonlanguage classes made a minuscule advance from 4.8 at the seventh grade to 5.3 at graduation. These are the classes to which the nonachievers, students whose reading skills are considered too poor for the study of a foreign language and who will therefore be ineligible for an academic program in high school, are consigned. In contrast, the remaining 50 percent of the students improved three grade levels during their three years at the school,. The implications of this survey are truly appalling. Students who are behind in reading have virtually no chance of catching up.

Why should this be so? It is not because Kennedy Junior High is an especially bad school. Comparatively speaking, it is probably superior to most of the 158 junior high schools and intermediate middle schools in the city system. Located in a middle-class neighborhood, it has long been known as a school for college-bound students, although that was more true some years ago before the adjacent neighborhood feeding into it deteriorated. Even so, it still can boast of a high proportion of successful pupils headed for the happy pastures of higher education. To all external appearances, also, it presents a picture of ideal racial integration with a fifty–fifty split between whites and nonwhites on the school register, if not in the ability-ranked classes. Although most of the nonwhites are from disadvantaged homes and make up the bulk of the nonachieving bottom half, many are from upward mobile middle-class and lower-middle-class families and do well in school.

No, as far as the disadvantaged students are concerned, we became convinced that the problem with Kennedy Junior High School is not that it is a poor school but that it is a junior high school, one that is run along traditional, bureaucratic lines. In other words, it is an impersonal factory in which students are treated as raw material in a continually moving assembly line. In a swift succession of forty-five-minute periods through the school day they shuttle to one class after another, each with a different teacher hammering away at a different subject in a sequence prescribed by tradition rather than the logic of understanding. In these classrooms the average youngster—and most particularly the youngster with learning difficulties—becomes lost in a mass of students seated anonymously in ordered rows. The emphasis is on subject matter, and the successful teacher is one who maintains order and covers the curriculum. Never mind if the students don't understand it. There is no room in the system for genuine remedial help and, except in exceptional cases, no room for a personal relationship between student and teacher. How could there be when each teacher is confronted with a moving parade of 150 students in the course of the day?

This is a learning and a social situation that imposes the

most taxing emotional and intellectual demands. The constant movement from scene to scene and the continuing need for readjustment calls for a high degree of ego strength, adequate intellectual skills, and a supportive home as backup. The middle-class children who come to school with these assets are generally able to cope with the stressful demands of the junior high school, though even they frequently experience difficulty, especially during the first transitional year.

For the disadvantaged adolescent, handicapped by severe academic deficits and with ego resources insufficient to integrate the shifting kaleidoscope of a junior high school day, the system is a prescription for disaster. These youngsters desperately need personal reassurance. In order to function they need a limited number of caring adults to whom they can relate in their school world. In order to learn they require unpressured time, the chance to continue at a single task instead of having to switch from one task to another. It goes without saying that they need massive help with basic reading, writing, and math skills and can only experience escalating failure unless their skills improve.

In view of the grotesque misfit between the reality of the junior high school regime and their pressing needs, it is no wonder that at this point so many of these youngsters give up all hope of making it. Instead, they become busy with self-destructive emotional defenses designed to make failure tolerable, which is why so many of them are referred for therapeutic intervention to the mental health agencies that serve them so poorly. This, then, is the "fraud" that is being perpetrated on the children of the poor.

References

Bard, B. (1972), , Schools get failing grade. *New York Post*, January 14, 1972.

Brenton, M. (1970), *What's Happened to Teacher?* New York: Avon Books.

Buder, L. (1972a), 60,000 truants linked to crime by school union. *The New York Times,* January 19, 1972.

———— (1972b), Scribner asks for improved instruction in reading. *The New York Times,* February 20, 1972.

Clark, K. (1970), Answer for "disadvantaged" is effective teaching. Annual Education Review, *The New York Times,* January 12, 1970.

Hechinger, F. M. (1970), High schools: Flunking grades for many of them. Education Section, *The New York Times,* November 15, 1970).

Hollingshead, A. B. (1949), *Elmtown's Youth.* New York: Wiley.

Hubert, R. (1972), The Duluth experience. *Saturday Review –Education,* May 27, 1972.

Katz, M. B. (1971), *Class, Bureaucracy and Schools.* New York: Praeger.

Larner, J. (1968), Crisis in the schools. In *Aspects of Poverty,* ed. B. B. Seligman. New York: T. Y., Crowell.

Maeroff, G. I. (1972), Career training: Learning how to make a living. Education Section, *The New York Times,* June 11, 1972.

Miller, S. M. (1967), The search for an educational revolution. In *Profile of the School Dropout,* ed. D. Schreiber. New York: Random House (Vintage Books).

Piven, F. F., and Cloward, R. A. (1971), *Regulating the Poor.* New York: Random House (Vintage Books).

Shanker, A. (1972), Where we stand, a weekly column of comment on public education. *The New York Times,* April 2, 1972.

Venn, G. (1970), Education is key to employability, Annual Education Review, *The New York Times,* January 12, 1970.

Weinraub, B. (1972), British find poor children lag. *The New York Times,* June 6, 1972.

CHAPTER 3 *The Problem Redefined: Arriving at the Therapeutic Classroom Model*

THE SPECIALIST'S-EYE view of a problem is, of necessity, limited, and the mental health professional is no different from any other in this respect. It seems that expert skills and knowledge must always be purchased at the price of a restricted perspective. As the distinguished physicist Robert Oppenheiner wrote: "In order for us to understand anything we must have to fail to perceive a great deal that is there." While selective perception leads to scientific discovery, it is responsible also for intellectual limitations. It is one good reason for the frequent failure of social programs based on perfectly valid scientific conclusions to produce positive results. Too many facts operating in the real life situation have been left out.

37

Closely related to the limitations inherent in the specialist's definition of a problem are the limitations imposed by the tyranny of conventions as to how professional service is to be rendered. The organization of services, the assignment of roles and role relationships, the control of resources and decisions, the recruitment and certification of personnel all tend to become locked into a confining pattern that cuts off even the awareness that more effective alternatives may be available. Only in the face of an urgent social and political threat are entrenched professional thoughtways and modes of operation subjected to re-examination and internal challenge, a process that is going on now in the field of education, although not so drastically as the headlines would indicate.

At the very outset our decision to offer mental health services on an informal, as-needed basis within the confines of a school rather than in a separate mental health clinic setting represented a break from professional patterns. Presented with an open mandate to reach troubled adolescents in any way that promised results, we were making a radical departure from respected therapeutic conventions. What was to prove most radical about it, however, we did not anticipate: it was not the changed mode of operation but the change that took place in our thinking. Encountering at first hand crucial factors not visible before provided new perspectives on the disordered behavior and emotional difficulties of adolescent school failures.

In effect, we were forced into a redefinition of the problem that pushed beyond the limits of the mental health perspective to take account of the visibly inseparable links among psychological dynamics, academic deficits, and school environment. This was a three-dimensional reality confronting us daily in our efforts to help students within the school setting, where the difficulties were occurring and the interrelationships were particularly acute. The redefinition of the problem demanded a different approach to its solution and led in a step-by-step progression to the concept of the therapeutic classroom.

Initially, a number of reasons had led us to break with convention and set up shop in a school. It was 1967. Adolescent drug abuse, academic failure, and school disruption had assumed serious proportions in New York City, and the alarm signals were up. While wider social and economic issues were obviously implicated, the major focus of the problem seemed to be the schools where youngsters spent more of their working hours than at any other place.

Working in and through the schools, therefore, seemed to offer the best possibility for reaching and helping them, especially in light of convincing criticisms that charged the impersonal public school system with failing to meet and indeed exacerbating student needs. It seemed that one important contribution we might make would be the creation of an opportunity for students to form close relationships with reasonable and sympathetic adults within the context of the school itself; that is, we would provide them with a special friend and advocate who would help them to negotiate the school system and to cope with personal problems. We expected that a significant windfall would occur in the form of an improvement in the general "climate" of the school.

What really decided us to make the move, however, is the inability of conventional mental health clinics to meet the needs of adolescents from low-income population. The model of weekly clinic visits makes demands that are beyond their capacities and fails to offer them a service that they recognize as meaningful. As we have pointed out, disadvantaged youngsters frequently refuse service completely or appear sporadically, usually when forced by the school. In the rare instances when appointments are kept, the once-a-week contact involved is so minimal as to make treatment peripheral to their lives. Furthermore, little is accomplished, because these youngsters lack the verbal skills for insight therapy.

Our plan was to conduct an informal, "drop-in" mental health service, emphasizing a generalized approach to therapy, rather than the working through of conflicts. To begin with, we called ourselves the Sounding Board in order to promote the view of the staff office as an informal place, in which students could talk about absolutely anything on their minds. Students did not have to come for regular visits or schedule appointments in advance. They were told that they could come alone or with a friend or a group of friends. Discussions focused on drugs, family difficulties, and the whole spectrum of adolescent problems. In addition, the Sounding Board had available the services of a psychiatric consultant whose speciality in short-term family intervention was used in cases where family therapy was indicated.

For disruptive, angry, and explosive students, lacking in impulse control, we assigned a worker who was available daily, whether for ten minutes several times during the day or for an entire school period. With these students the aim was to modify their behavior so that they would act more appropriately, with the Sounding Board worker serving as a role model or emotional anchor. In general, interventions focused on behavior modification, through the methods of reinforcement, support, reality-based interpretations, discussion, and ventilation. The aim was to effect a rapprochement between the student and his environment.

The involvement of teachers as therapeutic collaborators was central to our plans. Because it seemed that the teacher's role with the student would be tied directly to any gains, considerable Sounding Board staff time was spent working with and talking to faculty. We needed faculty help in understanding and diagnosing the student's behavior in the classroom. We also needed faculty help in carrying through each individual treatment plan, insofar as it was to be implemented in the classroom setting. It was hoped that some teachers would learn to work as part of a mental health team.

The Sounding Board got under way in Kennedy Junior High School in the spring of 1968. By the following spring the inadequacies of our program had become apparent, as had the need for a new approach. Presence in the school was not sufficient to touch the dynamics of students who were in trouble. A number of developments had led us to this realization.

In the first place, we were not reaching the target students: the chronically disruptive, the chronic failures, and the chronic truants. Essentially, we were still operating within the framework of the traditional, one-to-one relationship that makes demands that these youngsters could not meet, despite our openness and accessibility. Although we were not attempting insight therapy, we still needed to enlist the participation of the students in ways that were beyond their level of development. The students with whom we were succeeding, it appeared, were primarily those who could function relatively well academically or who could at least articulate their problems. The others were not prepared to discuss their responsibility for their actions, to think about the consequences of their behavior, or to plan ahead. With a number of them, we had to terminate treatment because our efforts were fruitless.

It became evident very quickly that students were suffering from learning deficits to a shocking degree. We knew that these students were in low-ability classes; it was not until we began to focus on the correlation between problem behavior, academic deficiencies, and resistance to therapy that we realized how minimal their skills were. Almost all   41 were reading many years below standard, and many could barely read at all. The poverty of their informational resources was extreme.

In the late spring an incident occurred that opened our eyes to the scope of these deficits and marked a turning point in our thinking about the problems with which we were attempting to deal. Several ninth-grade "problem" girls had been sent to the Sounding Board office for disruptive behavior. It turned out that they were worried about a test on the American Revolution the following period. Dr. Holmes, who was in the office at the time, sat down with them to review the facts. It soon became apparent that the girls knew nothing of American History, despite their having sat through classes dealing with the subject. They were not even sure who had fought the Revolutionary War. One girl thought it was the British and the English. Another thought that there were colonists involved. The rest were not sure enough to guess. It was suggested that they open the textbooks they were carrying and check. It then became apparent that the material in the book was so far beyond their reading ability as to be meaningless to them.

As evidence of this kind accumulated, we became certain that problem behavior was closely linked to learning deficits. In some cases we could see that the behavior constituted an adaptation to the pain and discomfort of failure and an attempt to avoid the label of "stupid" by taking on the more acceptable label of "bad." We started to speculate that possibly the best service we could offer these youngsters was to make it possible for them to improve their skills and, consequently, their self-esteem.

The junior high school structure could scarcely promote such positive change. The school was organized in a way that encouraged continued failure and difficulties. Passed on from year to year without mastering rudimentary reading or math skills, these pupils were subjected to a course of study that was thereby rendered incomprehensible. It was an *Alice in Wonderland* situation, a charade. Even in the slow classes the capacities of students were not equal to the demands being made. To avoid the trauma of exposure, they engaged in various kinds of denial, pretending to be engaged in impossible learning tasks or avoiding them altogether. At the same time the teachers were occupied with what we started to call "pretend teaching," that is, presenting unprepared students with assignments with which they were incapable of dealing.

It also became apparent that it would be almost impossible to deal with the students' classroom behavior, and to deal with teachers on a consultant basis, unless the students' behavior were seen at first hand. It is one thing for a teacher to describe student behavior, it is another to be present when it occurs. The third-party role in effecting modification of behavior was intrinsically inadequate. In point of fact, our initial hopes of enlisting teachers as collaborators were turning out to be Utopian. Most often they resented our involvement or felt that we were undermining their authority.

Another factor that sounded the death knell for the Sounding Board as an approach was the small scope of anything we might hope to accomplish by helping individual students at random. What appeared a potentially greater contribution would be the creation of a model of service for adolescent school failures that would have some impact on their difficulties as the present models do not. We were sure that such a model would have to involve a different kind of school experience, a change in the school environment that would take into account the interrelation between learning deficits and problem behavior. We were not sure at all, however, what form it could take.

Then something happened that unexpectedly gave us the clue. A special reading group had been started as a minor   43 facet of the Sounding Board program. This turned into what was, in essence, a pilot project for the new model we were seeking. The group, consisting of six boys who were non-readers and also behavior problems, began to meet in late November. They met for two whole days each week, remaining as a single unit that worked with a reading specialist who was interested in psychological dynamics and was working with us as a volunteer.

Little more than a month later the boys were showing such dramatic change as to make it evident both to us and to the school administration that something important was taking place in that classroom. Reading had improved, and so had behavior. The prime example, a ninth-grader considered one of the school's incorrigible "public enemies," was suddenly not appearing in the dean's office at all. From an incidental academic service, we now began to think of the remedial reading unit in terms of an approach to an experimental class that would combine teaching with therapy. The pieces of the puzzle were fitting together, and its solution seemed to revolve around what it was that Linda Melnick, the reading specialist, was doing right.

In many ways it was a classic case of serendipity, unplanned and unanticipated discovery. The original idea had been for the remedial teacher to work individually with a number of nonreaders, using the Spaulding phonics method that had proved extremely successful with older students. Linda Melnick had recently completed a course in the Spaulding method that focused specifically on its use with the nonreading adolescents of the public schools. She could spend two days a week with us.

It soon became plain to her that in the time available little could be accomplished. The most she could hope for was to spend two individual sessions a week with each of seven youngsters, which would add up to a fruitless effort. There seemed almost no point in even making the attempt on that basis. In a Sounding Board staff discussion, an alternate scheme evolved. Why not get the students together in a group! If Linda Melnick could have a full day twice a week working on nothing but reading with the same children, she thought, she might stand a chance of making some inroads.

The students in the remedial group (all seventh or ninth graders) were reading at either the second- or third-grade levels, as measured by the Metropolitan Achievement Test. During a preliminary interview each had indicated a real interest in participating in the program. It was essential that this should be their own decision because, as Mrs. Melnick made clear in talking to them, they would have to stay together in one room for a whole day and would be expected to work seriously. It was something that they must want to do, or the project could not succeed.

The group included a mixture of seventh and ninth graders for the purpose of testing the effectiveness of this kind of instruction at different age levels. There was one Puerto Rican boy and one white boy, and the rest were black. All had been in contact with the Sounding Board previously, two of them for extensive treatment. Their numbers included some of the most serious behavior problems in the school, hence the school administration's quick assent to our proposal. The Sounding Board's remedial reading class was doing the school the service of taking seven disruptive students out of the regular classrooms for two days a week.

A description follows by Linda Melnick of what happened in the self-contained remedial reading class and continued for eight months during its initial year. It makes very clear why what she was doing was right, and why it furnished us with an operating design for a new model of service for adolescent school failures.

45

Long before I could begin teaching them how to read, they had to get to know me. They had to begin to feel there was a reason to pay any attention, to hope that they could learn something, to feel that they were not really stupid. They felt stupid. In school they had always been in the lowest ability classes, and teachers had always made them feel that they were not worthwhile. Interestingly, all of them remembered the fourth grade as the year when things went wrong, when the teacher had been unfair and they had flunked out. Every single one in their first interview said that he had been called stupid by his father or mother or someone who was important to him.

They blocked constantly. They were stubborn. They were angry. There was one boy who was extraordinarily bright and was furious that he had been kept back a year. He moved along very quickly in the beginning and then, suddenly, there was almost a cutoff. It became obvious that he was fearful of succeeding, because once he succeeded he would have to continue proving himself. It was easier just to remain in the same old pattern of failure and to protest that he was being treated badly. Each kid in the class had separate problems that had to be coped with, that came up as a part of teaching them to read.

The therapeutic side of it was more intense than the scholastic. It had to be. When we started, I had little idea that we would be spending much more time on the emotional problems that they had than on the Spaulding method. It was all rather subtle. Occasionally, a kid would say: "Are you a psychologist or something?" There were very rare, brief moments when you could work purely with reading and not run into a block almost immediately that showed up in various ways—lack of attention, tuning out, talking, excuses to leave the room.

It was a matter of constantly having to stop and pull back and being aware of where the emotional element was entering in. With only seven youngsters and myself together for that long stretch of time in one room, there was literally nothing that came up that could not be dealt with on the spot. There were constant group discussions going on. More than anything else, the time was spent in discussions, talking about things that bothered them or that had come up out of what we were doing.

The discussions covered the range of their experience and concerns. At one time we talked about their anxiety over taking tests, and that there were techniques to know about taking tests.

Another subject arousing intense interest was the question of how to treat children, whether or not it was right to punish them physically. Many discussions involved the subject of prejudice in one way or another. One of the most meaningful discussions had to do with what it really means to be "stupid," and who was really stupid.

Sometimes I would call a kid on his behavior in front of everybody and point out how his actions were affecting the whole group. Taking a clue from reality therapy, I said to almost all of them on one occasion or another: "I'm here to help you but I can only do so much. I cannot make you read or write. You have to want to do it." I made it clear that I was there to help them, that I was unquestionably available, but that whether or not they succeeded was their own responsibility. It made good sense to them.

I also made it clear that their behavior was their own responsibility, not only for their own good but for the good of the group. They objected to all rules strenuously, because there were so many of them. I tried at first not to have rules, but then I had to institute some, because otherwise it was chaos. If they broke the rules—if, for instance, they took food out of the room and munched in the halls—I gave them a very reasonable argument: "It's not allowed in this school to have food in the halls. We can eat in our classroom because we're special. If you break that rule and you're seen, I won't be able to bring food in, and you'll be doing yourself out of something you enjoy." If I knew a boy was acting up in other classes on the days when I was not there, I would corner him and say: "You don't behave that way in my class. Don't do it in other classes. If it's boring, take something and go to the back of the room. Don't waste the time." Or I put it on the basis of, "You are really threatening our class when you act like that."

I was very open with them. I had explained at the beginning that I had never taught before and that I had just learned the phonics method myself. I told them that I was a volunteer and that I was there because I wanted to be. As I got to know them better, I could come in on certain days and say: "Don't bother me today, because I'm very tired. I was dumb, and I stayed up too late last night." It was fine. They knew where I was, and they could understand it. It was all very frank and very informal. I started the day off by bringing in hot chocolate and doughnuts, and we would sit around for the first half-hour or so just eating and talking. That went on through the whole year. One of the nicest things that

47

happened occurred three weeks after we started, when one of the boys said to me: "Some of us were talking about the food, and we were wondering whether you are paying for it. We think that we should chip in."

A big problem as far as teaching was concerned was to find reading materials that were sufficiently simple and yet interesting enough to hold the attention of fourteen- and sixteen-year-olds. I ended up bringing in a variety of books and magazines, but none of them was really right. At one point or another we used *Life Magazine*, the *Daily News*, a book on sex, the *Hardy Boys* mystery books. Two of the boys became fascinated by a book of black protest literature that was actually way over their heads.

One boy had become interested in oceanography through watching television, and I found material for him on that. A Ben Shahn art book with accompanying text was a huge success, especially for the discussion that it stimulated. We did not always read as a unit. Usually, I would work with one or two students at a time.

I have been asked what effect our class had, what the results were in terms of the progress that was made. I find that difficult to answer. Reading scores did go up, anywhere from one to three years. Knowing what problems these youngsters have in taking tests, however, and how variable their performance can be I'm not sure how reliable an indication that is. More convincing to me, I was reading with the boys, and I saw a tremendous difference in their facility from the beginning of the class to the conclusion of the year. Some of them were starting to write coherently at the end, which they were not able to do at first. But I really don't know. I wonder if you can expect a great change to occur with kids at this age in such a short time.

What I think did happen was that the boys came away with a changed attitude toward themselves and toward the adult world. If nothing else, there was an adult with whom they had a different kind of relationship for a period of time during one year of their lives. There was someone who said: "Think something of yourself. I happen to think well enough of you to stick it out in this room with all of you for the whole year because I want to." I never gave up on them. I acted like a human being with them, which was different from any experience they had ever known in a school situation. In the end they were able to communicate, to speak up about their feelings and fears; they had lost some of their terror of failing; they were more accepting of authority; and they had acquired some sense that they could control their own lives.

What happened in the self-contained remedial reading group was consistent with the principles of milieu therapy and related to the weaknesses of the fragmented and disorienting junior high school structure and to the internal dynamics of junior high school failure. It seemed to place beyond question the need for a mental health component in any effort to remedy the academic deficits of troubled adolescents. Youngsters like these are too blocked by disabling defenses for learning to occur without active classroom-based emotional intervention related to their individual needs.

Several aspects of the "pilot project" seemed particularly significant. When the classroom presented a benevolent situation where they could succeed at tasks appropriate to their abilities, once-disruptive students became quite manageable and receptive to therapeutic guidance. Furthermore, the simplified, restricted environment of a small class and a continuing relationship with a single adult seemed to enhance their ability to focus. The most impressive outcome, even more than improved reading scores and improved behavior, was the effect of this relationship in giving the students a heightened feeling of competence and autonomy.

Against this background the model of the therapeutic classroom began to take on concrete shape. It would involve a radical restructuring of the school environment for students with normal potential, whose academic difficulties are interrelated with their emotional functioning. Simply put, its underlying rationale proceeded from the thesis that "good learning is good therapy," a proposition that follows from the fact that the successful acquisition of real skills and knowledge brings with it self-esteem and the courage to

49

discard self-destructive defenses and enter into a therapeutic relationship. Specifically, the following features were to be included in the therapeutic classroom.

A Simplified Milieu

Students would stay in the same physical location, in the same classroom, for at least four successive periods during the day. They would have fewer teachers, possibly only two for the four major subjects, who would be with them over double period stretches instead of the usual forty-five minutes. With acting-out children, a forty-five-minute period is insufficient for accomplishing anything academically or for establishing relationships. Ideally, classes would contain twelve students, but no more than fifteen.

A Teacher–Therapist Coalition

In addition to the teacher, who would deal with academic material, the class would be staffed by a mental health specialist, who would deal with emotional processes that obstruct learning. The therapist, trained to recognize the varying dynamics of a problem situation, would deal with it appropriately, either by the use of discussion and group processes or by an individual approach. The therapist's role would be to facilitate learning by helping to create an emotional climate conducive to the abandonment of maladjustive defensive maneuvers. In the process, as students saw the mental health specialist as someone offering them a genuine service, relationships would be promoted, leading, in turn, to more basic therapeutic intervention.

A Realistic and Flexible Curriculum

The curriculum used in the therapeutic classroom would be totally realistic, meeting each student at his actual level of skill and interest. For students with only meager reading abilities, the standard-grade curriculum is meaningless, helping to perpetuate their long history of failure and accompanying self-destructive defenses. In the therapeutic classroom the primary academic emphasis would be on the strengthening of reading skills. It would be essential to emphasize success experiences among students disabled by failure.

Informal Organization and Reinforcement

The classroom organization would develop from small groups, rather than following the traditional single-unit arrangement, which precludes the growth of relationships between students and teacher. An informal type of class structure would make possible the use of positive reinforcement, immediate feedback, and the kind of individualized emotional support these students require. In general, the class would be conducted along non-authoritarian lines, with discipline exercised through the pressure of group norms and the encouragement of inner controls rather than external threat and sanctions.

If it proved successful, the therapeutic classroom might provide a workable model for low-achieving groups throughout the junior high schools. The question now was how to get a chance to put it into practice and thus to find out how it would work.

CHAPTER 4

*The Academy Is
Organized:
A Case of Realpolitik*

*B*Y THE END of April we had written twenty-two
pages outlining the rationale and operating procedures for a
therapeutic classroom program. A "think piece," we called it
or, more cynically, a "dream piece." It seemed visionary to
hope that a complacent, rule-ridden public school system
would implement a proposal calling for such drastic shifts in
time-honored procedures and goals. We were asking for a
repudiation of the household gods. To abandon the standard
curriculum, for instance, would surely be regarded as an act
of sacrilege.

Our proposal required not only basic changes but a
willingness to invest material resources in the change process. To expect either change or support seemed to deny the

53

bureaucratic facts of life. It is no secret that the massive weight of accumulated and often unconscious self-interest offers tremendous resistance to change in any ongoing organization. The self-interest is by no means limited to, although it certainly includes, elementary economic factors, such as who gets what jobs, raises, or promotions. Possibly more potent are the intangible elements of prestige, power, and self-esteem, with their subtle links to established dogma.

As the events of the past decade have shown, change is not impossible to achieve. However, the inertia associated with the status quo must be overcome first. That is not likely to happen unless the entrenched leaders are faced with a threat they can neither ignore nor contain. Since their automatic reaction to unpleasant facts is to wish them away, it usually takes something like a hurricane to elicit a response to reality. When we first came to Kennedy Junior High in 1968, for example, the administration was able to assure us in all sincerity that drug abuse was not a problem among students, a conviction we soon found to rest on sheer illusion.

By an opportune coincidence, less than a month after we had spelled out our thinking, the hurricane struck. The establishment felt in jeopardy, the bars to innovation were down, and the therapeutic classroom was an idea whose time had come.

We won an assignment to conduct a therapeutic class-room experiment but with very little time to make prepara-tions. Classes were to start directly the following fall. Other conditions were also far from ideal. The program would be for ninth-graders instead of seventh-graders; class size would be twenty instead of twelve; teacher recruitment would be out of our hands. Nevertheless, we never questioned, grasp-ing the opportunity. As we saw it, the problem of adolescent school failure was too urgent to permit the luxury of waiting for innovative elegance.

The hurricane that opened the way for the therapeutic classroom had hardly come without warning. It grew out of the upheaval in the New York City schools that started with the teachers' strike of 1968 and came to a head in the spring of 1970, following the invasion of Cambodia. Then, as later, the upheaval was marked by disorders and racial tensions that surfaced throughout the system, especially in the senior high schools. In Kennedy Junior High many of the middle-class parents were alarmed by the widespread disorders, as well as by the school's changed black–white ratio. Disturbed by disruptive incidents that had accompanied the change in ethnic and racial balance, the parents had been pressuring the administration for protective measures. Then, in a high school directly across the road, a violent confrontation took place between black and white students that spilled out into the streets.

What had been persistent pressure now erupted into an explosion. A few days after the violence across the street, several hundred parents converged on the school without advance notice and, more unnerving to the authorities, without advance planning. It was a spontaneous outpouring, spread by word-of-mouth and triggered by fear. They were there to demand protection for their children. They wanted the troublemakers out of the school. If the district superintendent and the principal were unable to make the school safe for their children, they should resign; and the parents would see to it that they did. Speaking to the aroused gathering in the school auditorium, officials promised that something would be done.

A few days later wheels were set in motion for the formation of two special classes that would, in theory, remove potential disrupters from the school scene and at the

55

same time take the heat off the establishment. These were not yet our therapeutic classes. The Sounding Board was still to come into the picture. When it did, Dr. Holmes reported the situation in a memorandum written for the record:

Were it not for the following set of essentially political events, we would probably never be allowed to try out self-contained classes next year. Kennedy Junior High used to be an all-white school, often referred to as the "country club." During the course of the last few years, the black enrollment has been rising at a very rapid rate. This year the presence of a relatively large number of disturbed students, who were indeed extremely disruptive in their classrooms, has led the PTA to pressure the district office to form a separate facility for disturbed children.

The superintendent has taken the position that he would support a separate facility, if money were forthcoming to staff it with excellent teachers and adequate mental health personnel, but that he would not sanction the formation of a separate facility that will function as nothing more than a jail. Recently the pressure on him has grown more intense, and there has been a major movement to remove him as superintendent of the district. Because of his need to pacify the parents without compromising his own sense of integrity, he requested the school to form two "career guidance" classes.

Meetings in which we have participated have made it painfully clear how these two classes were formed. The superintendent, needing some panacea, apparently asked our principal to look into the possibility of forming two career guidance classes. Our principal, in turn, jumped at the idea of jobs as a panacea and directed his ninth-grade assistant principal to form two classes in the current eighth-grade, putting together two classes of twenty students each who might profit from leaving school each afternoon for a job.

Unfortunately, no one had paused to consider that current business conditions might make it impossible to find jobs for fourteen-year-olds. In addition, no thought had been given to the academic side of the enterprise. The whole push was to get the classes organized so that the parents could see evidence of action.

Before the Sounding Board even learned about the new

project it was a *fait accompli*. Like magic, funds had been authorized for extra personnel. Forty current eighth-grade students were officially on the class registers, with parent permission slips all signed and on file. Four teachers, who would have one less class on their schedules because of the assignment, had been chosen for the staff. In keeping with the emphasis on containing disruption, they were all men, and all were known for their ability to maintain order. The automatic decision to place the classes in the ninth grade had been made on the same basis. It was the older youngsters who loomed as the most serious troublemakers.

Faced with a threat impossible to ignore, the powers-that-be had taken steps to defend their position. How effective the steps would be was another question. As we discovered, both the administrators organizing the classes and the teachers assigned to them were uneasy about how things would work out and uncertain how to proceed. What would happen if jobs could not be found for the students? How do you deal academically with an entire group whose sole interest is getting away from school? The classes could turn out to create more difficulties than they were meant to solve.

More fundamentally, the job–study program neither offered nor attempted a solution to the underlying problem, the problem of learning failure. Nothing in the action taken by the establishment came near to tackling the real issues. Segregating supposed troublemakers by placing them in classes with no remedial component was rather like applying a band-aid to cure a broken arm, in itself a classic approach in institutional affairs. Neither was there anything innovative in the action. The Board of Education's Career Guidance Program had been in existence since 1958, when it was set up by the Junior High School Division as a way of dealing with "the many pupils who were over-age, frustrated, retarded in most school subjects and indifferent to education." It could not exactly be described as an untried program or a meaningful one.

The situation, however, was ripe for the acceptance of innovation for a remarkably simple reason. No one on the school staff knew what to do and a great deal was at stake. There was a conspicuous vacuum waiting to be filled.

The manner of our entrance was true to the *ad hoc*, unplanned nature of the entire operation. Students of bureaucracy will recognize that it demonstrates once again the strategic role of informal relationships and networks within a formal organizational structure. The entire event hinged on a chance meeting in the teachers' cafeteria. Waiting for her sandwich at the service counter, Arlene Friedman of the Sounding Board staff overheard two of the school's assistant principals talking about the new program and its problems. One of them, it developed, was the person in charge of it. Arlene Friedman had been our liaison with the school staff during the year and was now friendly enough with both the men to break in and ask what was going on. Over lunch, she heard the details of the career guidance program. Then she asked some pointed questions, and the following dialogue took place:

Question: Do you really think you will find jobs for these kids?
Answer: We can't be sure. We're worried about it.
Question: What will you teach them? Most of them can hardly read?
Answer: We'll just go along with the ninth-grade curriculum.
Question: Why not make it a remedial program and help them to make up their deficits?
Answer: That sounds fine, but these kids are too old for that. It's too late for them.
Question: We think you're wrong. They can learn if you deal with the emotional dynamics.
Answer: We're having a meeting on this the day after tomorrow.

Why don't you come to it? Write up your ideas and bring them along.

Two days later we presented the therapeutic classroom proposal, reworked for the ninth grade, to the school's top administrators. They were ready to be convinced. The chief point we pressed was changing the emphasis of the career guidance classes from jobs to remedial teaching, with reading the first priority. That was our basic condition, our non-negotiable demand. It carried with it two immediate corollaries: the use of realistic learning materials, which meant abandoning the ninth-grade curriculum, and restriction of the program to students with severe skill deficits. An incidental but important side effect would be a reduction in disorders and disruption, since learning and behavior problems go hand in hand.

In swift succession a series of meetings followed, during which we negotiated an agreement. Acceptance of reading as the primary emphasis came quickly. Our principal had already secured the reading scores on students in the program. Going over the lists with him showed that the great majority of these ninth-grade students were reading at a third- and fourth-grade level. He agreed that improving their ability to read would make much more of a contribution than sending them out on jobs. It was decided that the few students whose reading was near grade level should not be included in the program, even if their behavior was a problem. The cutoff point would be a reading score of 6.9, two grades below standard.

The curriculum issue proved more difficult and ended in a compromise. As could be expected, the school people found it difficult to relinquish their faith in a prescribed course of study. They saw the merits of our argument, but their thinking remained dominated by the conviction that education rests upon the accumulation of information. It was   *59* our contention that, on the contrary, for students without the most fundamental skills and motivation, education meant skill acquisition, rather than information accretion. In the end there was a mutual agreement to start with a total emphasis on reading and basic math, to keep the curriculum flexible, and to reserve judgment.

The most encouraging meetings took place with the teachers conscripted for the career guidance classes. Ideally, an innovative program should be staffed by volunteers committed to its principles. At a minimum they ought to have indicated some interest in taking part. How would these men react when radically different conditions were thrust upon them? It was even questionable how they would react to spending time at a meeting. Teachers at Kennedy Junior High were notably unenthusiastic about extra chores of this kind.

Dr. Holmes' report on the first of our meetings with the teaching staff is significant for several reasons. It shows the openness that does exist in the public school system when the situation permits. It also indicates some of the problems that were going to face us when the therapeutic classes were in operation.

Last week the four teachers, Sounding Board staff and Mr. Marchi, assistant principal in charge of the program, met for a double-period (ninety-minute) planning meeting in order to discuss the selection of students and the overall planning for the class. I regard this meeting as an achievement simply because it took place. A double-period meeting in the school is practically unheard of. This meeting was a tremendous success. The four teachers involved became very excited and enthusiastic, even to the point of volunteering to meet in the future at weekly intervals, on their own time.

We were able to convince them of some very important points, without which Sounding Board felt that these classes would be doomed to failure. However, it must also be noted that a number of points remain unresolved.

1. On the selection of students, we were able to convince them

that the program is suitable for only one type of problem student, the youngster who is capable of functioning normally but unable to do so in the present system.

2. We were able to convince them that the class must be allowed to remain in one room, instead of being forced to move all over the school.

3. We were able to persuade them that each teacher should be with his class for a double period.

4. Not only did the teachers endorse this unorthodox proposal, they were receptive to our therapeutic suggestions.

5. Perhaps most important, the teachers and Mr. Marchi have agreed to a weekly meeting throughout next year.

On a less positive note, there are two questions still hanging fire:

1. In the matter of curriculum, the teachers are willing to try an open-ended approach but reluctantly.

2. They are very concerned with whose role is going to be what in the classroom. They are obviously concerned about their authority, which is too bad but not surprising.

The therapeutic classroom program was now past the talking stage, and we plunged into the task of making preparations. Two more meetings were held with the teachers before the end of June, during which we tried to hammer out specifics. The teachers were about to participate in (and lead) a new kind of classroom experience requiring educational skills and social work techniques not normally part of teacher training. It was essential that they be involved in the planning and organization of the program and also essential that they be prepared to cope with a good degree of uncertainty. Many urgent questions would only be answered when classes began, including the ongoing relationships between teacher and therapist, the precise content of the curriculum, and the problems of individual children.

At the same time we were screening students in a race against time, since the school year was almost over. We had fought for and won acceptance of four criteria as the basis of selection: low reading scores, average intelligence, ability to speak English, and absence of organic impairment. The program was not to be a dumping ground for just any disruptive or dysfunctional youngster. There were children who would be unable to benefit from this kind of program because they were too severely impaired psychologically or lacked the capacity to function at an "Average" level of intelligence. There were also youngsters who would benefit from a remedial program using therapeutic techniques but might not be chosen ordinarily because they were not disruptive and therefore not highly visible to the authorities.

First we sifted through the students who had originally been placed in the career guidance classes, eliminating several whose reading scores were above the 6.9 cutoff point. To those remaining from the original group, we added a number of other students as candidates for the program. Several had been Sounding Board clients, others were suggested by teachers, guidance counselors, or the remedial reading teacher. Each of these children was given the Similarities, Block Design and Vocabulary subtests of the WISC. The first two subtests, which tap capacity for abstract thinking in the verbal and nonverbal spheres, are good measures of overall intellectual potential and are sensitive to organicity. The vocabulary subtest has consistently shown the highest correlation with school success and overall IQ.

We were looking for children whose Vocabulary score might be impaired, as it frequently is in disadvantaged populations, but whose Similarities and Block Design scores were "Average." In the absence of time in which to do more complex psychological evaluations, this served as a rough screening device.

In addition, each youngster was interviewed. There was a fifth criterion for inclusion in the program: a desire to participate. We wanted students who were willing to make a commitment to improving their skills. We explained what the purposes of the program now were, that it would concentrate on reading so that those who had never learned to read properly would at least be able to do so. We tried to show them the importance of being able to read and to do simple math. We asked how well they read and whether they really cared about improving. This was to be a class for students who wanted to learn and who were willing to work.

We also tried to describe the way the classes would be organized and conducted, emphasizing that they would be run differently from the way with which they were familiar. There would be social workers right in the classroom, people from the Sounding Board staff who were interested in helping students. This would be one class where the opinions of students would count and where they could say what was on their minds. We would do a lot of honest talking about problems of all kinds, and we would want their involvement. Now, while organizing the program, we were very much interested in their ideas about it.

Several students who had wanted to be in the career guidance classes in order to leave for jobs turned us down. They had no interest in our academic goals, and the program was no longer promising to find jobs, although we would still permit students who had jobs to leave for work in the afternoons. Most of the youngsters we interviewed said, "yes." They wanted to catch up, the plans sounded good, and they would agree to work hard and contribute to discussions. With a number of the candidates, those who had behavior records that promised trouble, we asked for an additional commitment. They gave their word not to fight, to attend school regularly, and to remain in the classroom. While this was clearly no guarantee of permanent reform, it established a point of departure for the relationships we would try to develop later.

A footnote must be added for the sake of accuracy. Not all of the students could be tested and interviewed in the short time before school ended. Several were, therefore, seen during the summer, and, as it happened, two never went through our screening process because we were unable to reach them. This omission proved to have important consequences during the following program year.

Preparations for the therapeutic classroom experiment continued through the summer. When school was ready to open the next September, this is how the plans stood:

The project was to be called the Academy in the hope of reducing the stigma of a remedial program. It was to include two classes numbering no more than twenty, each of which would remain in the same room through four morning periods. The rooms were to have movable chairs and desks so that a circle could be formed for discussions or the class arranged into small groups. Assignment to the classes had been made on the basis of reading scores. The poorer readers, some of them virtually nonreaders, were in Academy A.

During the morning Academy sessions, each class was to have only two teachers, who would remain with the class through two periods, one double period of English and social studies and a double period of math and science. Afternoon schedules would take in minor subject classes outside the Academy organization, shop, typing, art, and gym.

Members of Sounding Board would participate in the Academy classes on a set schedule. The staff would remain the same, including a psychiatric social worker four days a week, two psychology doctoral students who worked two days each, and the director who was in school once a week. In addition to our work in the classroom, we would maintain an office near the Academy classes where we could hold small group discussions and see students for private talks. As to our role in the classroom, it was solely to facilitate learning. It was neither our interest nor intention to teach—a position we would look back on with amusement and amazement very soon after the school year started.

Classroom disturbances would be handled from a therapeutic perspective, with emphasis on developing self-discipline rather than relying on external constraint. The curriculum would be worked out week by week in response to the needs of students and their interests. Initially, several weeks would be devoted to laying a sound base for reading skills, through teaching the phonics method that had been used in Linda Melnick's class. There would be regular weekly meetings of the whole staff and regular meetings and communication with parents.

When school opened we thought we were ready. In meetings throughout the summer we had laid out an agenda for the first two weeks and even had a point-by-point outline for a first-day orientation talk. We were well aware that, as the year started, many unresolved factors could present hurdles to the Academy program. This was an unrehearsed innovation calling for a revolutionary shift in procedures and attitudes by students, teachers, administrators, and by ourselves as well. The progress of the two classes would be fraught with difficulty. The classes might, however, provide the basis for a new model of education that could be implemented in other schools.

CHAPTER 5

The Road to Relationships

*A*SKING THE Academy students to trust us was asking a great deal. Why should they take the risk? Why should they abandon the safety of their defenses for us? We were on the spot to prove ourselves, but at least now we had a chance. The flexible and intimate organization of the therapeutic classroom was giving us new opportunities for establishing our credibility. Here a complex interplay of factors could operate that fed into each other and, ultimately, brought most of the students to see us as genuine allies. Then, once we were accepted, they themselves sought us out, bringing their problems and feelings for our consideration.

With each student the story of how this happened and

when it happened is different. In some cases the breakthrough came almost immediately; with others it was the culmination of many events. The factors decisive to the breakthrough varied, too. We had started with the premise that helping students to improve their skills would be the key that opened the way to a relationship of trust, but the process turned out to be considerably more complex. With some youngsters academic success was indeed the key; with others it was one factor among several; with still others it hardly contributed at all. While the denouement of the stories was the same, the elements of each plot differed according to the character of the chief protagonist. At the same time there was a common theme that ran through all of them.

One way or another, the factor that built positive relationships involved our meeting a strongly felt need that the students were able to recognize at some level. In doing so, we became for them people of value and good will. All in all, this process took place in four fairly distinct areas where our role was visible.

First, we were their advocates in connection with school problems, coming to the rescue in suspension proceedings, run-ins with teachers, and fights with other students. Second, we gave them frank information and advice about their most conscious, anxious, and immediate personal concerns regarding sex and sexual behavior. Third, we helped them at long last to reverse the academic deficits that marked them as pariahs, a service that they came to acknowledge as their denial mechanisms were abandoned. Fourth, and less obviously, in our minute-to-minute behavior we offered them tremendous emotional rewards.

The students were given recognition as people. Their feelings and opinions were treated with respect. At the end of the first week, Sounding Board wrote the following concerning Academy A:

Doris was the most willing to verbalize her feelings. She was able to say that the class was "stupid," and then later she confronted me with a basic contradiction that she was right about. Doris told me that I had said I wanted the kids to tell exactly how they felt, but when they complained about the phonics method, I got mad saying they weren't giving us a chance. Rightfully, Doris accused me of giving them a mixed message, and I agreed that she was right.

One of the social studies reading groups had been scheduled for a test, but when they met, Janet Geller surprised them:

I first made an announcement that we were not going to have a vocabulary test as I had told them. I said this was due to Marlene's speaking up. Marlene felt that having all of their vocabulary words on a test was just too much. I stated that I had thought about it further. Not only did I agree with her, but I felt that having a vocabulary test was unnecessary altogether. It was good that she let me know what was on her mind.

One of the boys had been almost half an hour late returning to class. Mrs. Friedman took him aside:

I explained that when students were extremely late for class it was due to one of two things: (1) Either they wanted to get into a great deal of trouble because of something they were feeling; or (2) they were trying to tell the teacher that something was not right with the class. Kenneth immediately agreed with the second alternative. I tried to do a little role playing with him, with me taking the part of the student, and said that his job was to say, "Mrs. Friedman, this is really too easy for me and I'm very bored." I assured him that my response would be, "I'm very glad you could tell me that. Now I'll try and find some work that's harder for you."

The students were not only met with respect but also with understanding and concern. When Barbara appeared to be depressed throughout a whole period, Susan Jaffe reported:

69

I offered her the chance of talking or for me to go away. I did not want to intrude to the extent that she felt pushed, and yet I still wanted her to know that there were adults around who were concerned and interested. After a brief talk, which was mostly on my part, with monosyllabic answers on her part, I told her that I would leave her for a while and would be around to talk anytime she wanted to.

When Thomas acted listless and uncoordinated during the reading period, Janet Geller spoke to him after the class. This is how she described it:

Thomas seemed pretty out of it today. He had trouble pronouncing words that he usually is able to do. I asked him whether he was feeling sluggish due to some medication, letting him know of my observation. He told me he was taking medication for his asthma.

When Roger, a boy with college ambitions, became downcast at a discouraging evaluation of his progress, Susan Jaffe offered support:

I spoke to him for quite a while. I explained how it must be very difficult to sit down and try to read, when he's got all of these fears and feelings in his mind. He said that when he does read, he gets very upset when he doesn't know something. I tried to explain that if he would accept the level at which he was reading, without worrying about all these other things, he would be surprised that he would be able to read better and understand more.

When Arthur seemed to be looking for attention during a period break when other students were talking among themselves, Arlene Friedman went over to him: "Arthur was looking for a great deal of attention during this free time and I went over to talk to him several times. Toward the end of the period he voluntarily for the first time came over to me and shared a little bit about what they were discussing. I felt it was an attempt on his part to reach out in a more positive way with which I was pleased."

70

There was constant reinforcement of positive behavior and reassurance about abilities and worth. Progress was praised, effort was praised, good behavior was praised, not just in an offhand way but with a "big fuss," as Janet Geller put it. Understanding and empathy were praised. Letters of praise were sent home to parents. When Harold graduated to a more advanced reading group, an announcement was made with a flourish to the entire class. Janet Geller reported: "Harold was to enter Mr. Harris' group today, and Mr. Harris made an announcement to the class welcoming him in. Harold was very pleased. I used his leaving as motivation for the rest of the group and they all responded to this."

When Fay expressed some perceptive insights about difficulties she was having with a friend, Susan Jaffe commented:

At the beginning of the period Fay and Maria were involved in some kind of an argument concerning the fact that Maria is always bragging to Fay. Before we began reading, Fay made the comment that perhaps we all need to stop and look at ourselves. Things that Fay said indicate that she is quite perceptive and sensitive in personal relationships and at the end of the period I told her how I felt about her sensitivity.

When Barbara's parents received a letter complimenting her good work, the effect was unmistakable:

The other girls were negative and unenthusiastic, but Barbara was bouncy, positive, and a real joy to have in the room. She was willing to learn about anything that I wanted to teach and told me so quite explicitly, despite the fact that this put her in a somewhat uncomfortable position with her peer group. All of which speaks to the question of how much good positive reinforcement really does in a situation, and I guess that the answer is that it does a great deal of good.

In addition, we communicated our sincerity and our 71

regard for the students by exposing our own feelings with openness and honesty, reaching out to them on a person-to-person basis. When Mark was having difficulties with a rigid teacher, Janet Geller told him about similar experiences she had gone through in school. When Martin was persistently disruptive in Arlene Friedman's reading group, she asked whether he disliked her, as his behavior appeared to indicate. With unashamed feeling, Marvin Harris told his class about the funeral of a friend who died of a drug overdose. Janet Geller's report described the incident:

Marvin Harris told the class about the funeral he went to yesterday, which was the funeral of a friend of his who was twenty-three years old and who died from an overdose. Marvin was very open and honest, and the kids were listening intently. Marvin said that, initially, he was not going to tell any of his kids about this, but after going to the funeral he was moved and so depressed that he thought he would let them know. His friend was a twenty-three year old college graduate who was a teacher. His reason for taking heroin was because of the "kicks involved." Marvin said that he wasn't hooked, that he didn't take it all the time, that he didn't have to rob and steal. The problem with his friend was that he was "too smart." He thought that he knew everything and that nothing was going to happen to him. He went on to say that his friend died on Tuesday, and , of course, he never suspected what would happen to him. He had plans for the weekend just like all the kids there. And then he wound up dead. Marvin made an extremely dramatic presentation. He talked a little bit about the mother, telling how hysterical she was, how she kept jumping into the grave and crying, that she wanted her son to have another chance. He said that he was very moved by the experience. After Marvin was finished, he asked if anyone had any comments or questions. A couple of kids asked him a few explanatory questions. Somebody asked why Marvin didn't stop his friend. Maria and Kenneth began to almost accuse Marvin of not helping him. Fay was the one who was sensitive enough to this to tell them to shut up and stop acting as though it were Marvin's fault. It was really a beautiful discussion, and after Marvin finished I wound up having a small group that wanted to discuss this further.

A gifted teacher confined to a lockstep curriculum in a conventionally organized classroom can often manage to relate to students on a human level. Even so, that in itself is not enough to build up the kind of trusting, one-to-one relationships that the Academy made possible. Without a flexible agenda, small numbers, and team staffing we would not have been able to bring about such relationships, simply because we would not have been able to meet our students' needs. As it was, we could respond instantly and directly to emotional cues; we could allow spontaneous discussions around personal concerns; and we could organize special groups and programs, such as the sex education classes that laid the basis for a lasting closeness between students and Sounding Board staff.

We like and trust people who make us feel good about ourselves and who show that they understand and care about our feelings and fears. We are more apt to lower our guard with people who are open with us, because that makes the exposure of self less unequal and threatening. On another dimension, when people give us assistance with a stressful problem, we are likely to value them and be ready to move toward a greater closenesss. At best, something like an exchange occurs.

There was no reluctance on the part of the Academy girls toward receiving frank and explicit information about sex. From the first session of the sex education classes that Arlene Friedman conducted over a six-week period, extending into the first week of January, she had the absolute and complete attention and cooperation of every girl. Very soon after the Academy started, it had become obvious that the girls were anxious about, and preoccupied with, sex. It was also obvious that they were painfully ignorant about the most elementary physical facts and that their attitude toward themselves in connection with sex was extremely negative. One day some of this came out during the girls' reading

73

group in Academy A, when Arlene Friedman was working with them.

Marlene was complaining of not wanting to work. Finally she was able to say that she had been very nervous about something, but now she wasn't. With a little prompting she admitted that she had just gotten her period. I asked if anyone knew why they got their period and was astounded to find that not one of the girls had any notion as to why this happened to them every month. All of them had a great number of negative feelings about their menstrual period, but no one knew what it was all about. They all seem to worry about whether or not they will get their period, and part of their anxiety seems to be based, at least at first glance, on not understanding how one gets pregnant.

The sex education classes were held two times a week in the Sounding Board office. They started off with a scientific lesson on female anatomy and menstruation that deliberately emphasized the technical aspects in order to relieve embarrassment. At one point Arlene Friedman got down on the floor and did stomach exercises to show how menstrual cramps can be relieved. During the next six weeks the girls received very explicit information on conception, pregnancy, and contraception. As it proceeded, Arlene Friedman inserted what she called "propaganda" around the theme that sexual intimacy requires the context of a good and meaningful relationship. Making no claim to being neutral, she simply presented her own values regarding mutual respect and responsibility. It was an important perspective for the group to have, because these were girls with very little sense of their own worth.

The effect that the classes were having on how the girls felt toward Arlene Friedman emerged about two weeks after the classes began. She opened the period by announcing that they would discuss contraception.

They seemed very eager and anxious to go into this. I brought up the question of deciding when to have children, and I expected this would be an introduction into planned parenthood. Instead, the girls took off on this and thought I was referring to girls of their own age and teenagers. We began talking about their own experiences and about boyfriends. This was the first time that they had at all opened up with me. They talked about love, unwed motherhood, about knowing how to kiss, and the kind of man they would want to marry. The girls were really involved in what they were saying.

I thought that the group went really well and that my relationship with the girls was quite solid at this point. They were able to work together and enjoy each other's company. I also feel that there's a lot of good feeling and mutual trust on both sides.

Responding to the students' personal concerns was a matter of tuning in to available cues and following through. Both were possible because of the small size and flexibility of the Academy classes. It also had a great deal to do with how we saw them, with the therapeutic outlook that kept us constantly aware of the emotional component of their behavior. On a less subtle level, the students could count on us when they ran into trouble. Since it was our understanding with the school that we were to have a role in any disciplinary action that involved them, we could really help.

For the Academy students, trouble in school assumed various forms, with which they were thoroughly familiar. They were old hands at trouble. There was nothing new about having run-ins with teachers, referrals to the dean's office, fights, or even suspensions. This year, however, we were there acting as their advocates, helping them maneuver out of tight spots. We not only interceded for them, served as buffers and intermediaries, but showed them how to deal with unpleasant and unavoidable situations in ways that served their own best interests—how to "negotiate the system."

In addition to four periods in the Academy, most of our students went to afternoon classes in nonmajor subjects like shop, art, and typing, where teachers used a traditional, authoritarian approach and, as an apparent result, often had difficulty in maintaining order. In these classes youngsters who were typically reasonable and cooperative in the Academy context would find themselves unable to control their anger and frustration. Time and again we had to move in to cool off a crisis. A teacher would send for us, the dean would call us, the students or their friends would send out an SOS. Coming into a class for other purposes, we would frequently discover one of our students in a confrontation with the teacher. A report by Janet Geller shows the Sounding Board in action on one such occasion. Bruce, a model student in the Academy, had been accused by his typing teacher of stealing some supplies, and the teacher was about to send a referral to the dean.

Bruce was very upset because he didn't steal any supplies and because he hasn't had any referrals this whole year and doesn't want even a single one. Bruce attempted to explain all this to the teacher and eventually just blew his stack. He threw a chair and really began to shout that he was being accused wrongly. I tried to quiet Bruce, putting my hand on him as he was shouting and telling him to calm down. As Bruce shouted, the teacher shouted back, escalating the whole situation. I quickly told the teacher to let me handle it, and got Bruce out of the room and into my office, where he immediately calmed down. I pointed out to him the futility of arguing and getting angry at teachers. He told me he knew that it does no good to try and argue with teachers, but that he's very upset about being accused of something he hadn't done. I supported him completely but let him know that he was to let me handle this. I told him that there is a difference between an adult talking to an adult and a kid talking to a teacher and that not many teachers will back down with a student. I said that if ever again he were to have any difficulty with the teacher, he was simply to walk out of the room and come to my office. Bruce agreed completely. I left him in the office and attempted to straighten things out with the teacher, who agreed not to send the referral as well as stating that he believed Bruce did nothing wrong. I told the teacher that, as regards the three Academy boys in the class, I am always in my office, right across from him, and that he should feel free to call me if any problems come up with them.

Helping the Academy students in their run-ins with teachers was not always that simple. Sometimes it required considerable negotiating at both ends, as in the affair of Richard's letter of apology. Richard, with a long history of disruption complaints, was making great strides in our program both academically and in his behavior. We were, in fact, very proud of him. Unfortunately, he was still incapable of dealing with rigid teachers and was facing serious disciplinary action because of an incident with a teacher on hall patrol. It was an excellent, if depressing, example of the mutual blindness that produces clashes between authoritarian adults and egocentric adolescents.

According to Miss Bradley, Richard was inexcusably rude and had to learn his place. Unless he wrote an apology, she would press charges against him for threatening her. According to Richard, Miss Bradley should not have pushed or spoken to him as though he were a criminal. If he wrote an apology, he was afraid it would be used to humiliate him. Stepping in as an intermediary involved some delicate diplomacy. We secured Miss Bradley's promise that, once the apology was received, the matter would be completely forgotten. We worked with Richard on a letter that allowed him to keep his pride. The letter read: "Dear Miss Bradley, This is to say I'm sorry for what happened on that day. This letter is speaking for me as my apology to you. I'm not used to saying 'I'm sorry.' Richard Wilson."

Fortunately, while the faculty included its quota of arbitrary Miss Bradleys, the administration and most teachers were willing to accept our approach to crime and punishment, as far as our students were concerned. A number of tense situations were resolved successfully through three-way meetings in which we managed to effect a detente between teacher and student by making it possible for them to communicate with each other in a reasonable way. Program changes were accepted. Most impressive to the students, suspension terms were modified. In the case of Tony, who had been in a fierce fight, we persuaded the administration to reduce the suspension period to one day. In the case of Frank, who had lost control and punched an abusive girl after extreme provocation, the school agreed to keep the suspension off his cumulative record.

As it happened, our students rarely got into fights either inside or outside of class. Without any question they would have done so, were we not around to help them avoid confrontations. This was particularly the case among the girls. From the age of about twelve to fifteen—the junior high school period—many girls from poverty neighborhoods become embroiled in physical combat that often takes on the aspects of a gang war. Some of the Academy girls had done a great deal of fighting in the past. Now they wanted to avoid it, because they saw themselves as young ladies who were beyond that stage. When a challenge came up, however, they were at a loss for an acceptable way out. Nothing we did for them evoked more gratitude and earned us more trust than the negotiations we conducted to ward off fights.

One clear sign of the girls' reaction was the change that took place in the way that we learned a fight was brewing. In the beginning we had to find out for ourselves. Then the students started coming to us directly. One morning in late February Janet Geller was taken aside by several girls in Academy B. She describes the incident in her report:

> When I came into the classroom, Angela, in a friendly tone, told me to "pull up a chair and have a seat," because she wanted to talk to me about something. I sat down between her and Sylvia. She wanted my "advice," she said, and told me of the possibility of a

fight between her and Margo who is in class 9–12. It seems that Margo was being put up to fight Angela by another girl who used to be close to Angela and feels snubbed by her.

I asked Angela if she wanted to fight and told her I was glad she said, "no." I suggested that all the people involved meet in the office, and we'd try to work it out. Both Angela and Sylvia thought that was a good idea. Angela seemed quite relieved to have my help and patted me on the leg, saying I was "a good friend."

Developing relationships was a day-to-day, minute-to-minute process that went on continuously throughout the year on the several fronts where we were meeting the students' needs. This does not mean that the needs were always acknowledged or that help was immediately accepted. While we felt that reversing academic deficits constituted the greatest immediate need, most of the students at first did not agree. Their defense mechanisms were constructed to allow them to deny the pain of failure, of being "stupid." With many it was not until we had reached them through other channels that they could permit us to help improve their skills. With others, in contrast, it was a breakthrough in learning that laid the foundation for trust.

Richard Wilson was a boy with minimal reading and math skills whom we reached very quickly by lavish attention and approval that gave him the impetus to make dramatic improvement. Alton Wright was a nonreader who fought our efforts throughout the year, but whom we won over at last as he finally, unbelievably, began to read. Karl's story falls in between. Plodding along in the slow reading group for several months, he started to open up and make progress as our realistic expectations and support enabled him to concentrate. One of the most striking conversions occurred in the case of Harold, who started the year in the lowest reading and math groups while creating major behavior problems in the class.

About a month after the start of school, we decided to try 79 reaching Harold on a one-to-one basis. Mrs. Friedman called him out of his afternoon shop class and sat down with him in the Sounding Board office where, she reported, they proceeded to have a "nonconversation conversation."

By this I mean that Harold was completely unwilling to speak to me, and so we conversed for the first fifteen minutes by my asking questions answerable by yes or no, and he responding by shaking his head. I was able to tell him in multiple-choice form (nod your head to indicate which of these three answers is right) that I liked him and was choosing to spend this period with him because I wanted to help him. All this time he was staring off into another direction, refusing to look at me. When I asked him if he wanted to learn how to do subtraction, he turned and faced me for the first time and nodded his head, yes.

I sat down next to him and asked him to do a problem. It immediately became clear that he was attempting to do subtraction by working from left to right and that he had no notion of the orderliness of subtraction. I explained this to him and then suggested ways of borrowing that would make things clearer, so that he could really see what he was doing. He worked with a great deal of enthusiasm and spirit, and we spent the entire period working very hard. By the end I could say that he understood subtraction.

It was exciting to see Harold's sense of confidence grow as we continued. I kept making the problems longer and harder and telling him how much he was learning, and he seemed to take real pleasure in his growing skill. As a technique for finding numbers I used his street address and my street address and his telephone number and my telephone number and every other combination that I could think of. When we finished, I wrote glowing remarks at the bottom of the page.

Now that he had learned subtraction, he was jumped ahead to the most advanced math group and from then on he was like another person. There were no more behavior problems, no more tantrums about working. There was no more need to be disruptive in order to deny failure, because Harold was no longer a failure. In addition, he was now a cooperative member of his class who looked to us as people who were on his side.

As the relationships between the students and ourselves became stronger, the Academy program took on a different look. By the spring things were happening that would have been inconceivable when the year started. A boy who had initially resisted all efforts to let us teach him to read was now working eagerly with Janet Geller. A hostile, close-mouthed girl was asking for advice about her most intimate problems. Several of the wise guys who had refused to be serious were confiding their difficulties at home. A former troublemaker with a chip on his shoulder was trusting us with incriminating information. Youngsters who had started out angry, doubting, and belligerent turned out to be sensitive and anxious to learn.

Students were coming to us for help. They asked us to see them about problems that were bothering them. They asked us to work with them and complained that they wanted more attention. They crowded into the Sounding Board office in the afternoon just to spend the time. There was a closeness and honesty on both sides that was reflected in what we were able to accomplish academically, therapeutically, and in behavior control.

There were two or perhaps three students with whom we did not establish our credibility, whom we failed to reach. Possibly we needed more time, possibly it was too late for them to establish a positive relationship with any adult.

The students whom we did reach realized what was happening, and some of them were able to say so. At the end of May the daily report describes the following event.

Bruce came into the office while many of the kids were there and we were all sitting around. He approached me and told me that if there were anything that he could do for us next year he would be glad to help. When I asked Bruce what he meant, he said that if we wanted anyone to talk to the new students about the

Academy, we could count on him. I asked him what he would say about the Academy and told him to pretend that I was a new student and that he was coming in to talk to me. Bruce had some very positive things to say. He felt that because there was individual attention he was much better able to get the help he needed. He said that his parents had been very proud of his achievements this year, as he was. He also stated that he thought all of us were very nice and gave good consideration to each student. What particularly impressed me about this is that it was completely voluntary on Bruce's part.

CHAPTER 6 *The Road to Reading*

BY THE END of the Academy year almost all of the thirty-seven Academy students were reading and enjoying books for the first time in their lives. It was the real thing, a visible phenomenon—a point that bears stressing in light of the general skepticism about what can be expected from youngsters like the Academy students. ("You can't get these kids to read. They won't do it," teachers at the school told us.) Yet, by February, we were seeing: "Everyone was sprawled out, lying on desks, sitting on the desks, sitting on window sills, and reading, reading, reading" (Daily Report, February 8). "In Academy A, virtually everyone spends the entire period reading. The girls have their heads in books, and it is often difficult to get them to stop" (Daily Report,

February 24). Furthermore, we were hearing: "I told Barbara the period was over. She looked up from her book plaintively and said, 'Please, Mrs. Friedman, can't I finish this chapter?' " (Daily Report, February 5). "Some people read a book that would affect them, like the Helen Keller story, and they said, 'Wow, that was a sad story.' They liked it. It was good" (Marvin Harris, English and social studies teacher, Academy A).

They were reading easily and with pleasure and understanding, which we knew because they read aloud to us and talked over what they had read. It was happening with students who had started out with skills so inadequate and self-confidence so shattered that being asked to read anything loomed as a major threat. It was happening with teenagers who had never imagined that a printed page could have any meaning or interest for them, who had never understood why anyone should bother to open a book if they didn't have to and told us so in no uncertain terms.

This doesn't mean that all of the students were engrossed in "great" or even "good" literature, although some were. Nor does it mean that the majority of them—some with third-grade reading skills at the beginning—were working with highly complex material, although a number might have been. If one was reading a modern classic like *Native Son*, another was glued to sensational fiction like *The Godfather*, and a third absorbed in *Too Bad About the Jones Girl*, which was a simply written story about a pregnant teenager that was a great favorite. Finally, it does not mean that there were no exceptions to the general involvement. As a matter of fact, in different ways the exceptions are important in that they highlight the problems that must be resolved by a reading program for adolescent nonreaders.

As long as they were reading and finding pleasure in it, we didn't care what they read. We were not concerned about content, and we were not concerned about the acquisition of information, not at this stage, not yet. Our academic goal, which may sound modest but was actually Utopian, consisted of nothing but to have these fourteen- and fifteen-year-olds reading with sufficient facility so that they did not have to attend to the basic mechanism of sounding out each word. Without that ability they were unable to function in the schools now and would be unable to do so in the future. Year after year they had been presented with work that went far beyond their level of skill, that, therefore, they could not master. The consequence was accelerating failure, which only mounted higher as the complexity of curriculum material increased. Right now, for instance, their reading deficits put the standard ninth-grade curriculum hopelessly out of their reach. We proposed to forget the curriculum and to put first things first. Getting the students to read easily and with pleasure was our paramount, non-negotiable academic goal.

Like many investigators whose findings challenge the conventional wisdom, we did not realize then that others were arriving at similar conclusions about reading and school failure. At that time and in that place the idea of suspending the standard curriculum and concentrating on reading skills seemed wholly original to us and fairly heretical to the school staff who remained skeptical throughout the year. It was, therefore, a heady experience to unexpectedly find our thinking confirmed in a book that came out the following fall. Quite independently, Herndon (1971), had arrived at the same decision about what should go into an academic program for junior high school nonachievers and for almost the same reasons.

We decided that we would teach reading because the kids couldn't read well, and because you had to be able to read in America in order to be equal. We decided to teach only that, in order not to diffuse things, in order not to pretend that things were important that weren't. We knew that we, The People, didn't give a damn about Social Studies or DNA or the rest of the kit and caboodle of junior high academics. (If a particular kid really did, he could learn about it, now or anytime). We decided that the whole purpose of the time the kids spent with us would be to teach them to read well (pp. 129-130).

Just the same, while our paramount academic goal was the improvement of reading skills, we considered that as a means to another end. Basically, we were mental health specialists whose professional commitment is to help individuals with psychological disabilities function as whole human beings. Such a level of functioning is impossible for a young adolescent who lacks rudimentary reading skills, either while in school, when his deficiency pushes him into self-destructive emotional patterns, or later when it will cast him as an untouchable in the underclass of postindustrial society. We were concerned with education not as education but as a requisite for mental health.

However, as the reading program got under way we found out that in practice the distinction was irrelevant. One of the students, a girl initially so frightened and so unsure of herself that her lips trembled when she tried to read aloud, forced this realization on us early in the year. At first this girl completely refused to cooperate. "You can't teach me anything," she said, "which I don't want to learn." The lesson was clear and became clearer. Whether program objectives are educational or psychological, fifteen-year-olds with serious learning deficits must be dealt with on both fronts, if anything is to be achieved on either. In the Academy reading classes, teaching strategies and therapeutic strategies intermeshed so tightly that to describe them separately would distort the picture beyond recognition.

Experience in the Academy indicated the basic ingredients that must enter in some proportion into a model for teaching adolescent nonreaders to read. Teaching, however, is not the right word, and to talk of reading as a separate entity is misleading. The essence of the model as it developed was that it involved a dynamic process and that the process operated on the level of realistic needs. It was a process that included many elements, some more and some less central to it, ranging from specific procedures and techniques to the cumulative growth of trust.

Instead of attempting to spell out a system, the best way to explain the Academy reading program and the model it introduces is to train a hypothetical camera lens on the classrooms and describe the process as it occurred. Remember that we will be viewing two different classes in each of which two adults are working with the students. One is an English and social studies teacher and the other is a member of our Sounding Board staff of mental health specialists. As it happens, both of the teachers are men and we are all women. The classes continue through two regular school periods in the same room, and they differ both in ability and ethnic composition,. Academy A, with a roster of twenty, is made up of students who are officially reading four, five and six years below grade level. Of the twenty, two boys and two girls are white, three girls and one boy are Puerto Rican, and ten boys and two girls are black. The students in Academy B read about three years below grade level on standard tests and make up an unbalanced ethnic group. Of the seventeen, five girls and two boys are black, one girl and two boys are Puerto Rican, five boys and two girls are white (four of these boys are from Italian backgrounds).

The Phonics Failure

The first two weeks of the Academy year offer an object lesson in how not to teach reading to nonreading adolescents. Starting off with a thorough grounding in phonics is to be the first item on our agenda. This time there will be no more pretense about what the students can do. None of them possess the elementary competence in decoding the printed word, which is a prerequisite for reading with comprehension. The phonics system that they are to learn will provide them with the tools for doing just that. Reading for content will come later.

We don't plunge right in. First there are class discussions, open and honest on our part and theirs, or so it seems. We explain exactly why it is important that they acquire the fundamentals that they have never had the opportunity to master. We tell them that this is their chance to catch up and that they are all capable of doing so. We tell them that they won't have homework or textbooks and that once the phonics are out of the way we will work with any subject or material that interests them.

We ask them how they feel about the idea and whether they have any suggestions about how the class should operate. Everyone seems eager to go ahead. Considering how new this kind of open, informal discussion is for them, surprisingly many participate. No one objects to starting out with phonics. A few think that maybe they should have textbooks, because after all they are in the ninth grade. We explain that we are against textbooks until they can read. We remind them that in this class no one will pretend.

The phonics lessons start, and, almost immediately, like a powerful reflex, the students resist them. The Sounding Board report for Academy B on September 19 tells the story:

Mr. Schwartz began the phonics lessons today. Within a very short time after beginning, I noticed that about four girls had their heads down on the desk. They were not paying attention. In addition, several of the boys started talking, and others were looking out of the window. I pointed out to the class what was happening and asked them to begin talking about it. Without any hesitancy, one of the girls whose head was on the desk began to say that she thought this was baby stuff. The others quickly agreed. They were verbal and very agitated. One of the girls agreed that she needed help in reading, but she still objected to the method being used, and she felt that this class was for dumb kids.

The lesson that is coming through turns out to be one that is for us, and it concerns the true nature of realistic teaching. Of course, we should have realized it before. We were asking the students to take on a task that is such a blow to their self-esteem that it is unrealistic in terms of their emotional needs. They are psychologically incapable of handling it, despite the logic they have accepted beforehand. We try for a while longer to work with the phonics system, but the complaints keep mounting. The work is babyish; the class is stupid; they should have books and homework like other ninth graders. One day a student insists on keeping the door shut so that people passing by in the hall will not see what the class is doing. A little over two weeks after it started, the phonics system is dropped in both Academy classes.

Reading in Groups

We are in Academy A with the poorer readers, and it is the beginning of November. The English period is about to begin. The students are still fooling around after the between-period break. Mr. Harris raps on his desk with a ruler. "OK everybody. Let's break up into groups."

After some urging and a little more fooling around, the twenty youngsters have settled down into four clusters, each sitting around a table. One group of eight boys hold xeroxed copies of a newspaper article about a professional basketball game. All seven girls are together around a table with copies of a letter from an Ann Landers column. The other two groups have different books from the Hardy Boys series.

For the rest of the period each group carries on as a separate unit following a similar pattern, with students taking turns at reading aloud. There are, however, differences. In the group that Mr. Harris works with first, the reading is slower with much more laborious sounding out and explanation of word meanings. These are the poorest readers. He leaves them to continue with one of the students as leader and joins the second Hardy Boys group where the students are reading with much less hesitation. Here each one goes through a paragraph, and then the next explains what has been read. In the meanwhile, the larger group with the sports story is busy doing very much the same thing, reading aloud to each other, looking up vocabulary, and explaining what has been read, but they are also doing a great deal of talking and arguing about the game that they are reading about and the players who took part in it.

Of all the groups, the girls seem most engrossed. They have started out reading the Ann Landers letter and then have become very much involved in what advice should be given. The letter is by a girl who likes a boy and doesn't know how to attract him. There is an animated discussion of what she should do with much disagreement and considerable reference to personal experience. Arlene Friedman from the Sounding Board staff, who is sitting with them, joins in the discussion. Then she distributes the answer that actually appeared in print. They read it, and another discussion ensues. Mrs. Friedman now gives them a second letter to read and moves off to work with a boy who has been sitting on the fringes of the slow group.

The Academy A reading groups have taken shape in the weeks following our decision to give up formal classes in phonics. Forming the groups in Academy A has been a simple process, requiring little preparation beyond drawing out the students on the kind of material they would like to read. When we did that, a natural breakdown occurred almost automatically, undoubtedly helped by the friendship networks that were operating. The girls were all enthusiastic about getting into romantic problems; some of the more grown-up, athletic boys declared their chief interest to be basketball, and the others quickly agreed on mystery and adventure stories. Varying ability levels have posed no problem, except in the large mystery group, which include some students who could barely read. For that reason we have divided it into two sections.

Procedures in the groups center around reading out loud, which discourages skipping unknown words and difficult passages. Many of the students enjoy doing it and clamor for their turn. For others, the hiders, reading aloud has been a threatening experience, forcing them into a painful exposure. Throughout the proceedings we give them a tremendous amount of encouragement and praise, and this has made it possible for almost all to take the risk. Hand in hand with the reading go various techniques for developing comprehension. The students explain what they have read, look up words that are strange to them, and answer questions in writing about the material. As the groups continue, we develop more devices, including crossword puzzles and word games. Reading groups will continue in Academy A in various forms into the spring.

The *Chico* Breakthrough

Joe Cardone is an oversized fifteen-year-old who prides himself on being tough. On the subject of reading, his views have been loud and clear. Reading is for sissies. He has never read a book and has no intention of starting now. "What for? I just wanna be a carpenter." Yet now, in the middle of November, Joe, like the other Academy B boys, is sprawled out with his nose glued to a book called *Chico* (Swinburne, 1968). He and they are reading it silently and with such absorption that we decide not to break in.

Up to this point the program in Academy B has been floundering. Getting the students to work has been tremendously difficult, and we seem to spend most of the time dealing with resistance and disruptive behavior. A major factor in the situation is undoubtedly the animosity that has surfaced between the white boys, who are openly prejudiced, and the black students, most of whom are girls. We have been taking class time to hold separate meetings with the two groups in an effort to dampen the tension. Try as we will, Academy B will not settle down into reading groups. The boys, with a standard "wise-guy" attitude take it all as a big joke and an opportunity for horseplay. The girls are more willing to try, especially if the material brings up personal issues they can talk about, but, more generally, they refuse to participate because reading aloud is "babyish."

An even greater stumbling block has been our failure to find material with which the students will be willing to work. The trouble is that stories and articles to which they can relate are too far beyond their capacities to produce anything but frustration and a reaffirmation of their "stupidity." The material that they can handle is geared to a childish level that insults their dignity.

Chico seems to be different. This paperback book of 123 pages is explicitly written for junior and high school students with reading disabilities. It is crammed with dialogue, profusely illustrated, and features a sixteen-year-old hero from a poor background. Chico is a half-Irish boy from Puerto Rico who wins out over the dangers and disappointments that confront him in New York during a reunion with his long-lost, convict father. Three elements are prominent in this story: first, Chico's quick-witted courage, independence, and competence; second, his defiant challenge to a rejecting father, who subsequently reforms and recognizes his son's worth; third, the high concentration of suspense in a quick-moving plot whose main outlines follow the familiar format of crime stories on television.

Never mind that it is not fine literature. The boys are reading *Chico* with comprehension, fascination, and concern, reading it without stop until they are finished and then talking about the story to each other and to us. On November 20 the report for Academy B includes the following: "The entire class was beautiful today. There was really a relaxed atmosphere and everyone was working. Some kids were reading *Chico* with feet up on tables and in earnest concentration, others were sprawled out on the window sills. Frank was engrossed in writing a composition on *Chico*. Joe and Tony were telling me about *Chico*." It is the first book he has ever seriously been interested in reading, Joe Cardone informs us.

What we have to know is why. What is the magic formula that has produced such a dramatic breakthrough? A combination of rewards is the answer, we think. One of the rewards is our approval and attention, which have come to matter by now. Another is the good feeling of being able to read with comparative ease material that they don't consider childish. The real payoff is the pull of the story itself, which presents a fantasy world that meshes with their own.

The Sports Group

Last night the Knicks won over the Hawks, and the boys in the Academy A sports group are jubilant. Marvin Harris comes over with a big grin on his face—he's a Knicks fan, too—and hands out copies of Joe O'Day's story in this morning's *Daily News*. The headline reads "Knicks Roll, 128–119; Pete Pops 40."

"Just the same, we'd better not start celebrating yet," Mr.

93

Harris says. "Wait till you read how Pete Maravich played last night. If he gets any better, we're in trouble."

The boys have immediately started poring over the score box, which is printed next to the story, and are arguing with each other about how the different players have performed. Kenneth Mansfield, who is the group leader and the biggest of the bunch, shouts them down.

"Come on, let's get going. Who wants to read first?"

With Marvin Harris sitting among them, the boys take turns reading aloud from the newspaper report. Several of them read slowly and cautiously but with obvious relish, making spontaneous comments on what they are reading in the process. One of them gropes his way with difficulty, and Kenneth shows him how to sound out some of the words. As the reading proceeds, the boys get more and more upset at what the writer has said about the star of the rival team. Mr. Harris sympathizes, but tells them they have to face facts.

"Listen. This guy Maravich is good, and he's just beginning."

He tells the boys that he's going to bring in a magazine article about "Pistol Pete" Maravich for them to read tomorrow. Now he wants them to take paper from their folders and write a paragraph listing the strengths and weaknesses of the Knicks and the Hawks. While they are doing that, he will work with another reading group. As Marvin Harris gets up, he asks the boys if any of them want to shoot some baskets with him after school. Kenneth and three of the others arrange to meet him in the yard.

From its start in late October the sports group has functioned well, maintaining the continuing interest of some highly unlikely candidates for a successful learning program.

A number of factors have helped. Most of the boys are from the same neighborhood and hang around together outside of school. They are big, strong boys, and athletics is the one area where they feel comfortable and competent.

In addition, a special relationship has developed between the boys and their teacher. Marvin Harris is a young man in his early twenties who played basketball as a student and is as enthusiastic a sports fan as they are.

Reading about sports was the boys' idea in the first place, and they are quite willing to work together, long after the other Academy A reading groups have given up reading in rotation and taken up individual books. All through the basketball season the sports group follows the Knicks, reading newspaper stories that appear before and after each game, as well as articles about the star players. For a couple of weeks there is much excitement about a magazine contest that offers prizes for predictions about the final outcome in the two basketball leagues. After the basketball season is over, the group gets into other sports and athletic events, including the big Muhammed Ali fight.

Interestingly, though their reading skills are poor and the material they are reading is fairly difficult, they have no trouble understanding the general content because they are thoroughly familiar with the context. Specific words are something else, though. Marvin Harris underlines the more literary and unfamiliar ones for the boys to figure out as the reading moves along. Watching the sports group in action as the year progresses, it is apparent that the boys are enjoying what they are doing. At the same time they are reading more than they ever have before.

The Book Market

It is between periods, and two of the Academy B girls are chatting outside the room. Janet Geller from the Sounding

Board staff stops when she sees them. She is carrying five paperback volumes in her arms.

"Barbara, I've got a fantastic book for you about a black family. I know you're going to like it. And Marilyn, I didn't forget about *Love Story*. Come on in. I'll give them to you."

The girls break into broad smiles and follow her. Barbara grabs her book and leafs through it quickly.

"Hey, this looks good."

She goes off to a corner with it where another girl is already settled down reading *Native Son*. Meanwhile, several of the boys have clustered around Janet Geller and she hands out the other three books. One is called *Cop*, another is *Born Free*. In each case she tells a little about the book and why she picked it for them. To one boy she gives a copy of a 1950s best-seller called *A Stone for Danny Fisher*.

"Frank, I went through three paperback stores looking for the kind of book you want, and then I came across this and I remembered it from when I was in high school. It's terrific. It's just for you."

Frank looks at the book doubtfully. "Gee, it's big. It looks hard."

"Never mind that it's big. It's good. You try it. Mr. Schwartz and I will help you with it. It's about a kid who grows up in Brooklyn and becomes a prizefighter and belongs to a gang. In fact, he goes to Erasmus Hall High School."

"No kidding." Frank has definitely become interested. He sits down with the book and becomes lost to the world.

One of the boys around Miss Geller who hasn't received a book is complaining.

"How come you bring books for everyone except me?"

"You should have asked. Aren't you reading that book about racing cars?"

"I'm tired of it. It's got nothing but descriptions."

"Well what do you want to read next?"

"I dunno."

"OK. Wait till everyone settles down, and I'll talk to you about it."

Janet Geller confers briefly with the Academy B teacher, Mr. Schwartz, and he turns to the class.

"Will everyone please get going with your books," he starts.

"I finished my book," someone calls.

"I don't like my book, I want a new one, " from one of the girls.

"Me too," another chimes in.

Mr. Schwartz holds up his hand. "All right. While I'm going around reading with you, Miss Geller will talk to everybody who needs new books and see what you'd like her to get for you. If there's time she'll take some of you to the library and see if you can find something there."

It is now the beginning of February, and the reading program in Academy B is booming, with students reading individual books chosen to fit their own interests and reading ability. During the period both the teacher and the Sounding Board member go over to the students one by one, listen to them read aloud, talk over the meaning of what has been read, pick out difficult words to look up, and at the end of chapters assign questions to be answered in writing. That part is easy. The kids love the attention that it involves, and almost all cooperate eagerly. What is not so easy is to find a book that will hold them.

After *Chico*, we know that it is possible, but we discover quickly that reading skills, motivation, and points of reference are too diverse for one book to do the trick for the whole class. *Chico* was a lucky find. Gradually we evolve a procedure through which we probe each student on what his interests are and what kind of reading material will appeal to him. At first, the students simply don't know what to say. They have no idea what might be in a book. But by now we have come to know most of the students fairly well. We understand where they're at emotionally and socially, and we are able to make suggestions that usually work, although not always. If the book we offer them lacks the pull to keep them working, whether because it's too hard or too easy, too remote from their experience or too close to it, we don't push it. We get another book.

During the process we scour paperback bookstores, school and neighborhood libraries, our own libraries, our own memories. Two of the most successful books with the girls in Academy A, who are also reading individually, are *17th Summer* and *Pray Love, Remember*, emotion-laden romances that one of the Sounding Board staff had read as a young teenager. Many of the books are written on a simple level, but many others are distinctly adult, and we learn that what makes one or the other appropriate is not necessarily the student's reading skills. There is a fine balance to be struck between material that matches ability, and therefore provides the gratification of a successful performance, and the more difficult material that answers an urgent psychological need and provides an emotional gratification at a deeper level. This dilemma has been brought home by the sight of Barbara plowing laboriously through *Soledad Brother*, with the aid of a dictionary in which she seems to be looking up every other word.

The problem of finding books becomes easier as a kind of ripple effect develops. A youngster sees his friend interested in a book and he wants it, too. When a kid really likes a book he tells the others about it. "You ought to read this book. It's really good," we hear one girl tell another. Some of the students go further and read the good parts aloud to a friend. At various times, both in Academy A and B, we have our own best-sellers that zoom in demand.

The Attention Factor

When experts analyze the reading process they usually identify two basic components: the decoding of a linguistic symbol and the comprehension of the symbol's meaning. In the Academy reading program, a third basic component enters—emotional nourishment. The nourishment comes primarily from our approving attention as students read out loud to us, one at a time, and as we engage in person-to-person exchanges that are strongly supportive. Emotional nourishment is also a key element in the small reading groups and in the interaction among students that develops from their reading.

The tremendous power of attention and recognition, especially for youngsters like these, becomes more and more apparent as the year advances. Everything that happens between the students and ourselves has to do with learning because it contributes to the cumulative growth of trust and the associated willingness to risk exposure. With some students this emerges early, while with others it is a gradual growth that is promoted by private therapeutic talks. There are several for whom such trust never develops: A non-reader remains unable to face the shame of his incompetence; two girls continue to be implacably unapproachable behind an impenetrable wall of hostility.

As time goes by, instead of waiting for our approach, many students take the initiative, pressing and competing for our attention. Others, more uncertain, wait to be coaxed and, then, blossom with our interest. Most significant for what it says about the role of emotional nourishment is the fact that some of the students will not read at all, unless we are sitting with them and holding their hands—psychologically and often physically. Responding to students with special needs, we find ourselves giving more attention to some students than to others; this is a dilemma that we have yet to resolve when the year ends.

Items from the daily reports show how the attention factor operates:

I talked with Marilyn about *The Little Prince,* which I had given her to read. While Marilyn said she liked the book, she found it difficult to understand. I decided to go over with her what she had read, and she was very receptive to this. When I asked her what the book was about, she was able to tell me, pretty much in sequential order what she had read (March 30, Academy B).

I called Marlene out of class in the afternoon to read alone with her in the office as we had agreed. As Marlene began to read, her hands and her voice were shaking. This girl is really petrified of exposing herself. I put my arm around her, sat very close to her, and gave her continual reassurance. As she continued to read, and as she found that she could read with a lot of help, she felt a little bit better and loosened up a little (January 4, Academy A).

Barbara has *Mr. and Mrs. Bojo Jones* and was very interested in the book. She was reading the good parts out loud to Angela and Sylvia, who were listening intently. It was a very good interaction, which was spontaneous and which led to a good discussion about marriage and what they all want from guys in terms of getting married and feeling loved (March 16, Academy B).

During class I called Angela over to discuss *Native Son* with her. I invited Arthur over and told him he could participate in our discussion. At first he said no, but when Angela said, "Come over here sugarplum," letting him know he was welcome, he joined in and we had a very good, appropriate, and fruitful discussion. We even got into a somewhat philosophical discussion of whether life imprisonment was better, the same or worse than death (March 1, Academy B).

What, then, are the ingredients that made the Academy reading program effective? One way of answering that question is to ask another. What elements of the operation were essential? As we see it now what happened would not have happened without:

1. Person-to-person contact between the students and ourselves, which is only possible in small groups or individual sessions and is not possible with front-of-the-room teaching;

2. Motivating material, which involves a fine balance between skills, interests and self-image, and varies with the child;

3. Emotional rewards, which are derived from the positive reinforcement of a trusted and attentive adult and which are therefore dependent on the development of a trusting relationship.

This is saying, in essence, that in order to produce meaningful results, the learning situation for adolescent school failures must be totally realistic. As Glasser (1969) has said, "There is only one place to start and that is—where they are" (p. 57).

It's a statement that is fine as far as it goes. It does not, however, go far enough. Dealing with "where they are" in terms of skills and information will not accomplish very much, unless "where they are" in terms of emotional needs also enters in. We now know, as we did not know originally, that a realistic learning situation has to take into account four separate but inter-related needs that are distinctive to the youngster whose school career has been an unbroken experience of failure and who is dominated by deep feelings of inferiority and powerful defenses against exposure.

The need to experience success—The teacher must assign tasks that the youngster can handle with his existing skills and information. This involves the elimination of pretend teaching, which forces the child to assume he is stupid, since the teacher's expectations for him seem so far from his capacities and, what's more, others can meet them.

The needs for self-respect—The great problem for a remedial program is the stigma it implies, which intensifies the denial maneuvers of vulnerable youngsters whose self-esteem is already too low to be bearable. Nothing is more unrealistic than attempting tasks or techniques that the students find degrading, realistic as they may seem in terms of skills.

The need for relevance—Somehow the material that the students work with and the tasks they are assigned must make a connection with the world of their significant experience, whether of fantasy or fact. In one way or another they have to find it "interesting"—which means involving—in order to learn.

The need for self-respect—The great problem for a remedial youngsters who associate learning with humiliating failure to risk themselves without the benevolent attention of an accepting adult who matters to them. Only when such a relationship has been established does real learning take place. It is for that reason that a realistic reading program for adolescent school failures will concentrate on building relationships as the first, indispensable step toward the accomplishment of its objectives.

References

Glasser, W. (1969), *Schools without Failure.* New York: Harper & Row.

Herndon, J. (1971), *How To Survive in Your Native Land.* New York: Simon and Schuster.

Swinburne, L. (1968), *Chico.* New York: McGraw-Hill.

CHAPTER 7

Therapeutic Discipline and How It Worked

*I*N THE ACADEMY program there were youngsters who were among the school's most serious behavior problems, and there is no doubt that for the faculty and administration our chief value lay in taking a good number of troublemakers off their hands. The question of discipline—of initial control—was paramount in our mind as we took over the classroom operation. We did not, however, "exercise discipline," and the term "therapeutic discipline" is, in a way, misleading. What we were involved in was behavior modification.

To give an example from the daily record:

Mark Silvera was starting to act "high," running around the   103 room with a water pistol that he threatened to squirt at the kids who were reading. Mark is a boy with little impulse control who finds it difficult to focus unless an adult is with him. I tapped him on the shoulder and said quietly, "Remember our agreement:" Mark stopped short and nodded. He said "OK" and left the room. I followed him out and praised him for having the control to cut short his excitement and to leave the situation that was triggering it. He has kept his part of the contract that we made regarding his behavior. I asked Mark if he felt ready to go back. He said that he would like to wait a few minutes, because he didn't think he can settle down yet. I told him to sit outside with his book and to come back in when he has pulled himself together. I read with him for a few minutes and then asked him to continue by himself.

Or another example:

Doris Perez was angry and excited and refused to work with her reading group today. She seated herself on the window sill and banged her feet against the wall making loud, insulting remarks about me. At one point Doris picked up some books and hurled them to the floor. She screamed violently that she hated the class and the teachers. She said: "Mrs. Friedman doesn't bathe. She smells. That's why I can't stand her." Neither I nor Mr. Harris reacted to what she was saying or to what she was doing.

One of the boys asked me, "Why do you let her speak to you like that?" I answered him in a loud voice so that everyone could hear: "Doris is only acting this way in order to get attention. She is capable of being a good member of the class, she has many fine qualities and abilities, but as long as she behaves like this the best thing to do is ignore her. If she behaves like the fine person she can be, then we will pay attention to her. Otherwise we will not." Thereupon, Doris grew quiet. She came down from her perch and pulled up a chair to the Ann Landers reading group, with which I was working. I asked her to read, which she did with considerable concentration. I told her she was really doing well and said: "Now tell us what you think of this letter. Your opinion is always worth hearing."

These, then, are examples of how behavior can be changed. Again, the process depended on the existence of a trusting relationship, on commitment, and on an understanding of basic behavioral dynamics. Particularly, one had to maintain conscious awareness of the feelings of frustration and discouragement that were the signal characteristics of the Academy children.

While the school staff was skeptical about what we proposed to do, they were more than ready to accept an offer that would make their job easier. We had every sympathy with their problem. Disruptive behavior is a serious matter that can make it impossible for a class to function and affects the climate of the entire school. It was our hope that in the Academy classes we might find an answer to the discipline problem through a therapeutic approach. This would be of service to both school and students. The disruptive behavior that was preventing the school from functioning was preventing them from functioning too.

Why did we think that we could succeed where experienced and well-meaning professionals desperately in earnest about finding a solution had not?

Simply, we were proposing to deal with problem behavior from a different point of view and with different methods, which we felt would have a different effect. We were proposing to depart from the traditional way of "exercising" discipline in the classroom. That is, we would abandon an approach that relies on the exercise of external control and visibly fails to work and employ a therapeutic approach aiming at the development of *internal* controls.

The two approaches are at odds, both in theory and practice. Let us say, for instance, that a group of students in a classroom have become excessively noisy or disruptive. The teacher has two alternatives open to him:

1. He can react in authoritarian fashion: that is, he can shout, he can threaten, he can stand and wait for silence, he can send students to be disciplined by others.

2. He can walk over to the group and ask them with genuine interest, "What's happening?" "What specifically is going on right now?" "Is there something the matter with which I can help?" This conveys the message: "If you are acting in this peculiar manner, I can only assume that something must be wrong. If something is wrong, I as your teacher genuinely want to help you."

The first approach does not work, while it seems that the second does—not immediately—but in the long run. Over a period of a few months real changes started to take place in the Academy classes. At the end of the year an Academy teacher was to say: "In a regular classroom you would just repress their behavior, in our classroom I saw these kids *change* their behavior."

Then why not simply abandon the ineffectual authoritarian approach and apply the behavior-modification techniques that promote the building of inner controls *and* self-discipline. Unfortunately, there is a problem with the use of such techniques. To use the therapeutic approach, the teacher must have a knowledge of the psychological dynamics that are involved in problem behavior, as well as of the techniques that can be used to deal with them.

More than that, even with this knowledge the teacher must be able to build a relationship with each individual student. The organization of the conventional classroom makes this extremely difficult if not impossible. Consider that usually a teacher is faced with thirty students whom he is attempting to handle as one undifferentiated entity and that he is operating by himself, alone. To conduct a lesson in the conventional classroom setting, a teacher needs quiet simply in order to be heard. Further, the evaluation of his competence will be based in large part on his ability to control his class, which means keeping them in their seats and silent.

In the Academy classes, with students working individually or in small groups, it was possible to carry on a consistent program of behavior modification, with immediate and continuous reinforcement of any evidence of positive behavior. When disruptive behavior occurred, it was possible for the Sounding Board staff member to intervene therapeutically on the spot, directing her attention completely to the individual or the group involved, because there was always someone left to supervise the rest of the class. This might mean taking out a single student or several students or drawing them aside within the class for private or group talks.

Because the curriculum was flexible and because there were two periods and therefore sufficient time available, it was possible to interrupt the class and conduct a discussion revolving around acting-out behavior. It was possible to devote a whole period away from the classroom to small-group discussions geared to therapeutic ends. Finally, it was possible to develop the relationships that are indispensable for the effectiveness of the therapeutic approach to discipline. The therapeutic approach will work only when children feel that they are genuinely liked by the teacher and that the teacher is actively concerned with them.

In the special setting of the therapeutic classroom, we could bring to bear on problem behavior a psychological perspective through which such behavior is viewed as a symptom that must be diagnosed and treated in terms of its underlying causes. A child who is disruptive, as well as the child who retreats by hiding in class or truanting, can be helped only if we can understand the reasons for such behaviors. The "why" of what he does, rather than *"what"* he does, is the crucial factor. Just as children steal for many different reasons, so they "disrupt" and "retreat" for many different reasons. When the "why" is understood, the particular techniques necessary to modify the behavior itself can be selected. This kind of understanding can only emerge over time. Similarly, it can emerge only in a context where the child can be perceived as an individual. Modifying techniques, then, can be implemented only in a context where each student can be related to as an individual.

It is disruptive behavior that commonly receives the most attention, simply because it threatens the ongoing operation of the entire class. One of our regrets is that in the Academy we, too, found ourselves focusing on the "troublemakers," to the neglect of children who were defending themselves in less disruptive ways. For the sake of the children there must be a resolution of a dilemma that promotes a situation in which the quiet child who desperately needs help is overlooked in favor of the disrupter who poses a more immediate threat. From the vantage point of a contribution to the critical problem of order in the schools, however, our preoccupation with the disrupters did provide us with an indispensable picture of the general patterns into which adolescent disruptive behavior falls.

In trying to conceptualize a classification for disrupters based on the underlying dynamics, Dr. Holmes suggested the following:

1. Adolescents whose disruption served as a smoke screen to conceal their academic deficiencies—The label "bad" they could accept; the label of "dumb" was unbearable. These are students who would rather be sent to the dean than risk themselves by answering a question when called upon by the teacher. Their disruptiveness is a protective mechanism used to ward off a damaging blow to an already impoverished sense of self-esteem.

In the Academy environment, they were relatively easy to handle. Here they could be protected from the possibility of exposure in front of an entire class, and they could quickly see that adults in the room were aware of their academic deficiencies, did not disapprove of them, and genuinely wanted to help them. In essence, we would say to these students: "I understand that reading is very difficult for you and that at this time you really are a very poor reader. This happens to people for a lot of different reasons. In your case it has nothing to do with your being dumb. I will be here to help you learn how to read, and with a lot of help from me and a lot of hard work on your part, I know that you can do it."

Once such a child risks himself in a one-to-one relationship, he very quickly sees a little bit of improvement and can go on to risk himself in a small-group situation. As his self-esteem increases, the need to mask his deficiencies decreases, and with it the disruptive behavior that has been serving this purpose.

2. Adolescents whose disruptive behavior is a device for gaining attention, like Doris Perez—We are all aware of the child who is hungry for attention and has learned that even negative attention is better than none at all. This is the child who acts in a disruptive way in order to avoid being ignored or passed over. The Academy environment made it possible for us to recognize these dynamics and to treat them with a program of positive reinforcement in which only expressions of positive behavior were noticed and rewarded, while negative behavior was studiously ignored.

The greatest mistake that can be made with such a child, a mistake that is made over and over again, is to move in directly and ask him to "stop" or "to be quiet," which means noticing him and "rewarding" him for misbehavior. The results of this attention will only be an escalation of the negative behavior, ending in a power struggle and confrontation. Similarly, if the behavior is not consistently ignored, what occurs is a program of intermittent reinforcement that makes the behavior even more resistant to extinction. Such a child will do anything to retain the focused attention of the teacher and, indeed, of the entire class. When he finds an alternate route to receiving the recognition he craves and discovers the old one blocked, this disruptive behavior disappears since it is no longer serving a useful purpose.

3. Children whose disruptive behavior is the result of an ego deficit in the area of impulse control—They are the ones with "a short fuse," the children who have virtually no frustration tolerance and at times are literally unable to control themselves. When a teacher acts to "discipline" such a child, it only makes the situation worse. If he shouts, threatens, or sends the student to be disciplined by someone else, this only raises the level of the child's excitability and does nothing to help him reestablish control. In the Academy classes, the problem of low frustration tolerance was common. The Academy structure enabled us to help the child to control his behavior before it got out of hand.

With such a child it is not enough to tell him that he must learn to tolerate frustration. He does not know how or why he is feeling and acting the way he does. Therefore, we tried to help him to ask: "Why am I acting this way?" and "How do I look to others when I behave this way?" As an intermediate supportive step we tried to teach these children that if something was too frustrating and they felt their control going, they should leave the situation that was upsetting and wait for help to arrive.

4. Children whose disruptive behavior arose out of lack of trust, an ego deficit in object relations—There are some individuals who do not successfully accomplish what Erik Erikson has described as the most important task of the child's first stage of development, which is the establishment of a basic sense of trust. They are extremely mistrustful of adults. Their disruptive behavior is an expression of their resulting anger with adults and is a maneuver to "get even." Before anything can be accomplished with such a youngster, it is imperative that a relationship of trust be established, that he or she discover that there are adults who care and who want to help.

In the Academy environment it was possible to build such a relationship with students in a variety of ways, as is discussed elsewhere in this book. When such a bridge of trust is built, it can transform the angry "troublemaker" into a constructive ally.

Unfortunately, it is also true that some of these mistrustful youngsters put up a wall that is extremely difficult to penetrate. We had several children in the Academy whom we were unable to reach, who remained suspicious of our motives, and who regarded all attempts on our part to deal with their feelings as an unwelcome intrusion by the "enemy." These youngsters would have been happier in a more structured, less open setting where they were not challenged to respond to overtures that they could only experience as threatening.

5. Children with an ego deficit in reality testing—In the Academy we had one student for whom the public school was not an appropriate setting. He should, in fact, have been in a residential treatment center. This was a youngster who lacked a firm sense of reality and failed, therefore, to have an awareness of the possible dire consequences of his behavior. When such a child becomes disruptive and is asked, for instance, to leave the classroom, he is placed in a position from which he cannot retreat. He feels omnipotent, that nothing and no one can control him. From a practical and a therapeutic point of view it is necessary to let the child know that he can, in fact, be controlled. For such youngsters, a call to the dean or to the security guard is often necessary both for the safety of the rest of the class and for that of the child himself.

With modification techniques tailored to the "why's" of each case, we found that many children considered beyond control were quite reachable and quite manageable and quite literally changed their behavior. In one sense this happened because of the special setting in which we were operating. In another sense it happened in spite of it. For youngsters conditioned to regimentation and to external controls, a looser situation with few punitive consequences for their behavior presents an almost irresistible invitation to challenge authority. To any educational reformer who might consider placing disruptive adolescents in an open classroom without including therapeutic treatment, our advice is—don't. The result will be more acting-out behavior and more testing of limits and heightened mistrust, as happened in the Academy at the beginning.

In the Academy classes students were allowed to move around and talk, as long as others were not disturbed by what they were doing. They were allowed to chew gum, an unheard-of depravity in the conventional schoolroom. They were allowed to bring food into the room in conformance with rules that were worked out in general discussions. In many unaccustomed ways, the class presented them with a situation for which they were not prepared. They were waiting to be reprimanded and threatened, to be told, "Do what I say because I'm the teacher." Instead, they were asked to offer their reactions, express their feelings, make suggestions. While some responded with immediate cooperation, the initial response of others was to become unruly or suspicious. "You teachers are being too nice," one girl student said in all seriousness. "I know there's a catch to it."

Internal controls must be learned, and the learning takes time. With children like these, controls can only be learned with the help of a trusted adult who is able to diagnose behavior, is knowledgeable about techniques for modifying it, and is in a situation where the techniques can be implemented. Before the Academy, we had reasoned that this must be so. Now from our experience we know that it is so.

The significant interactions involved took place both within the classroom itself and in the office that we maintained a few doors away. It was in the classroom, however, that the process started and that many key events in the process occurred. Stepping in as the behavior is going on or, hopefully, before it has intensified can produce immediate effects in maintaining order and lay the groundwork for deeper gains in the future. From the start of the year to its finish, on-the-spot interventions were continually taking place in the most assorted forms and combinations, depending on who was involved and what was happening.

For instance, one of the boys refuses to work and is shouting across the room with highly disturbing effects. We go over to him, bend down, and speak softly. "Why are you acting this way? Is something wrong? Don't you know that it's really disturbing everyone else?" This is a boy who is very responsive to reason. "I guess I forgot," he says. On the other hand, when two of the boys start acting silly and hide themselves in the closet, we ask them to come out and take them to the office. When several of the girls get started on a noisy argument, we draw them off to a corner of the room and get them to talk out their differences.

One of the devices we found effective was to establish very specific contracts with the students, setting up conditions for their behavior to which they explicitly agreed. Often the agreement was written down, and they signed it. Sometimes the contract committed them to regular attendance or to carrying out a specific task, an arrangement that can be helpful to the student who has a need for structure. Sometimes the contract involved an agreement to leave a situation that was proving to be intolerably frustrating. Many of the contracts stipulated that the student would speak to a Sounding Board member if something was bothering him. Contracts were treated as serious commitments by the students, and often a certain amount of bargaining took place in working out their details. "No," a student objected. "I don't want to say I'll come to school every day for the rest of the year. How about making it for two months?" One of the most important aspects of the contracts was that they involved the student directly and responsibly in the control of his behavior.

Group discussions centering on behavior or attitudes took place throughout the Academy year. In the beginning, particularly, the entire class was involved as we tried to make the students active participants in the decisions affecting them, rather than passive and resentful consumers. Many of them, for instance, were returning late from the between-period break and were using bathroom passes as a device for staying out of the room and fooling around in the halls—a strategy, of course, that is almost a tradition in the student culture. We asked the class to talk about why this kind of behavior occurs and to agree on rules concerning it. "What do you think should be done when a kid doesn't return to class?" was the crucial question to decide. Hardly to anyone's surprise, a wise guy immediately answered, "Shoot them." When we persisted, however, the students became very serious and came up with a highly reasonable solution.

At various times when disorderly behavior had gotten out of hand we called a halt to whatever work was supposed to be going on and held a discussion about the reasons for their behavior and our own feelings in connection with it. "Why are you behaving in this way?" we challenged them. "Have you thought of how it makes us feel when you do?"

Other group discussions took place in an effort to work through difficulties that involved a smaller number of students. They were usually held in the Sounding Board office, either on the spur of the moment when a problem came up in class or at a prearranged meeting. Noisy disruption, refusal to work, angry disputes, threatened fights—these were some of the situations that prompted the sessions. As the students grew accustomed to talking with each other in an honest exchange, they became increasingly adept at expressing their feelings and were able to accept the perspective of others. It was fascinating to see group processes, once set in motion, lead to a resolution of antagonisms and an understanding of motives. These youngsters were becoming increasingly capable of communicating with one another.

One- or two-time group discussions were adequate to resolve sporadic incidents, but the situation in Academy B, where simmering racial antagonisms had come close to the boiling point, called for more drastic measures. It happened in the middle of October. For over a month, we held separate meetings in our office with five highly prejudiced white boys and six bitterly resentful black girls from the class, first on a daily basis and then several times a week. Since they were held during class time, one function of the meetings turned out to be that they kept the two groups apart while feelings still ran high. Interestingly, while the racial tensions had already emerged as a serious problem at the point when the groups were started, these tensions were not the immediate reason for calling them together. In each case, we were responding to the request of an Academy teacher who was experiencing difficulties that seemed far removed from the race issue.

The same pattern emerged in both groups—white and black. The youngsters started out discussing the immediate behavior problems—lateness and disruption—that had been the original reason for calling them together and then quickly veered off into heated discussions of race. As a consequence of these parallel outbursts, the decision was made to continue the groups on a regular basis. The Sounding Board reports on the first meetings tell the story:

The boys—I met with five boys from Academy B on October 13 because of their constant disturbance in class. They started off with Joe, as usual, leading by saying that they don't learn anything in Mr. Schwartz' class. The boys expressed a great deal of dissatisfaction about this, indicating that was why they do so much talking.

Then Joe started talking about the racial problem. Mr. Schwartz had a discussion for two days regarding race relations. This infuriated Joe, who is quite prejudiced and found the discussion very difficult to handle. He did a great deal of ventilating about how he hates "niggers," and, how Mr. Schwartz should not permit the kind of discussion that went on in class.

Joe's initiation of this discussion resulted in the boys' going along with and agreeing with him. They got more and more angry as we continued to talk, with the windup being that they felt like "bashing a few heads." The bell rang at this point, and the boys went out with these angry feelings. I decided that I should really meet with these boys every single day until some of their feelings settle down.

The next day I called for the boys again to have another meeting. Once again Joe expressed his angry feelings against blacks. This time he called them "coons," "colored," "stupid," and "dirty." He said that he hates them for all of these reasons. I permitted Joe to express his feelings without any interruptions. He told me that he has been jumped by black kids on more than one occasion and that they have attempted to extort money from him. The other boys chimed in, with the exception of Mark, who tried to put in that it's not only black kids who are bad, but that there are plenty of white kids like that too.

The boys began to talk about the riot that occurred this summer. It seems that during the summer a bunch of black kids were jumped by a lot of white kids. Joe proudly told me that it was he and some of his friends who did it. All the boys thought that the riot was great because the blacks got the raw end of the deal.

The boys knew that I met with several black girls and wanted to know what I discussed with them. Mark was able to say that I wouldn't tell because it was confidential, but he thought that I was talking about the same thing with them, because black people were prejudiced toward whites, too. Frank wanted to know if I had told the black kids that the white kids didn't want to learn about black culture or were angry with them. I really had to assure him that I had done and would do no such thing.

Impressions and suggestions: These boys are very upset about the discussion on race that occurred in the classroom. I believe that for all of them there is underlying fear and hostility toward blacks, based on experience as well as whatever values their families have imparted to them. They are able to keep these in check as long as no one brings them to the surface. However, the minute that a discussion on race is opened up, the boys find it very difficult to handle and practically lose control. Of course, they get very anxious about this loss of control, which results in all the problems that we have seen—anger toward the teacher for permitting such a discussion, all of their angry feelings about members of another race, all of their stereotype impressions, and their tremendous fear that they are not going to be able to contain themselves, which they mask by bravado.

The girls—Mr. Marshall asked me to see four of the girls from Academy B with regard to a disciplinary matter. Like the meeting with the boys yesterday, this one turned into a ventilating session about race. We started off talking about their refusal to make up their lateness in coming to class. During this time Barbara sat in an angry silence. When I tried to draw her into the discussion, she burst out that the class was stupid, that the teachers didn't treat the students well, and that she was very angry at teachers and white people. Since Barbara was beginning to express her feelings, I let her talk.

She said that she was particularly dissatisfied with the discussion on race in Mr. Schwartz' class. She felt that he was prejudiced, and this was discussion that should never have taken place. Barbara stated that the schools always present blacks in a bad light. She said that she wouldn't mind learning about black people if this was also balanced with learning about white people. She felt that teachers consider blacks some kind of curiosity that needed to be studied.

Angela then said that she was very hurt and felt "bad" about what Mr. Schwartz said. She felt that she could "burst out crying." Barbara then volunteered that Angela felt hurt, because that was the first time this kind of thing was ever said to her. Barbara is no longer hurt by these statements, because she's become hardened to hearing them and is very angry about it. Both Barbara and Angela said that they felt like belting one of the teachers.

The bell was about to ring, and I thought it was important to summarize what had taken place. I let the girls know that I could certainly understand some of their feelings, and I thought it was important for us to continue talking about these angry feelings. I suggested that it would be a good idea for us to meet on a regular basis and attempt to talk these things out in the hope of finding a solution that was nonviolent. I stated that we cared about their side of it and about their feelings. Barbara agreed to this, although she felt that it would really do no good.

Suggestions and impressions: These girls are very angry and sensitive about the racial situation. As with the boys, there is tremendous underlying hostility and fear. It is important that the girls have an opportunity both to ventilate and to understand something about whites. Hopefully, through our group meetings, they will be able to work out and work through some of these feelings.

The long-range goals are for both groups to be able to talk out their feelings, and, when they are through ventilating, to be able to explore whether prejudice is valid.

Meetings with the boys continued longer than those with the girls, but a similar pattern occurred in the tapering off. After the sessions had been going on for over a week, both of the groups seemed to have exhausted their feelings on the racial issue and wanted to talk about other things, which they did. We are making no claim to a formula for resolving group conflicts. This is simply a report of what actually took place in a concrete situation. The groups met in intensive sessions; there was considerable ventilation of strong feelings; for the rest of the year they were able to survive together in the classroom without friendship, but at least without explosion.

There was also another outcome. While all this was going on, we were building relationships with the youngsters in the groups that opened the way to reaching them on a one-to-one basis in connection with behavior and learning as well. As the year progressed, there were more and more private therapeutic sessions with Academy students in general, both for purposes of behavior modification and as a result of behavior modification that had already occurred and made them available for further change. In the area of therapeutic discipline, as in the area of learning, the magic formula, mysteriously potent and tremendously complex, was a relationship of trust.

CHAPTER 8

Chronicles of Change—I

*A*N END-OF-THE-YEAR balance sheet showed a dramatic improvement in the behavior and academic skills of the Academy students. Truancy had become minimal in a group of once-incorrigible truants, serious disruption and fighting had ceased to be major problems, and most of the students were reading with interest material considerably above the level at which they had started. In addition, and not coincidentally, almost all of the students had formed genuine relationships with us.

The dynamics of change in the therapeutic classroom fell into a number of patterns. These are described in the following six case histories that pick up on the typical students introduced in the first chapter. In each case the   119 story is told by the member of the Sounding Board most involved in the details of what happened. Janet Geller, who spent four full days each week with the Academy students, tells the sagas of Kenneth, Frank, Doris, and Martin. Susan Jaffe describes the development of Barbara; Arlene Friedman tells about Richard.

Kenneth

He is a black boy from a ghetto neighborhood, tall for his age, physically powerful, a leader among his peers. In school he has a long record of discipline referrals, some serious. Teachers consider him threatening. Always in low-ability classes, he reads at a fourth-grade level. There had been no contact with the Sounding Board before this year.

Kenneth was a surprise. He started off in the Academy behaving as he always had—sitting back in his chair, talking while the teacher was waiting for attention, making wise remarks, ready for any opportunity to defy an order. There was the same hostility and mistrust, the same refusal to participate. He sat with his friends—a group of four or five kids who hero-worshipped him—fooling around, staring out the window or just sitting blankly while work was going on. He seemed to be waiting for a chance to spar with us in one of his familiar power struggles.

When I saw him acting up those first few weeks, I would walk over and say in a soft, nonthreatening way, "Kenneth could you get quiet now? You can see the teacher is waiting for everyone to get quiet." If he went on, I would say, "Come on, why not?"

Other times, I spoke to him in the hall. There were constant five-minute trips out of the classroom in the beginning, talking to Kenneth in the hall. "What's going on?

Why are you acting this way today? Are you mad at somebody? What is the teacher asking? Is it such a big thing to be quiet?" Sometimes he would start walking. Lots of times kids walk around in circles or move away when you're talking to them. I would say, "Hey, I'm talking to you. Do I have to chase you?" He would come back, and he would listen.

It always worked. I never had any trouble reaching him. I'm sure that if I had used the exact same words in front of the whole class, it would have been a different story. Then, with the other kids watching, he would have had to look like a big guy and save face.

Any amount of reasoning with him worked like a charm. This occurred to me when I said to him: "Why do you talk when the teacher is speaking? How can you hear what he's saying?"

"I can hear," Kenneth replied.

"If you can hear, what did he just say?"

Kenneth repeated the teacher's remarks word for word.

I said, "You're right. You're one of those people who can talk and listen at the same time. I can see why you feel you can do it. But it creates a disturbance for the other kids to whom you're talking and for the teacher who's trying to get heard by the class. So even though you can talk and hear at the same time, please, don't."

And he stopped.

Gradually, out of these contacts a relationship was building between us, something that Kenneth had never allowed to happen before with an adult in that school. It was a relationship of mutual respect. Could you call it a therapeutic relationship? Not in orthodox terms. Kenneth was a classic example of an adolescent who would not have cooperated in insight therapy. Nor did he really require it in order to be helped to function. We were not working

121

through Kenneth's problems with him but dealing with them concretely as they occurred. We were also changing his environment, offering him through his contacts with us a different kind of experience with adults.

At the same time that an understanding was growing between Kenneth and myself and other Sounding Board staff, the same thing was happening with Marvin Harris who was the English and social studies teacher for Academy A. Marvin is a young man in his early twenties, a former basketball player and great sports fan, who very much related to students on a man-to-man basis. Kenneth liked that and responded to it. When the reading groups started, Kenneth and his friends decided they wanted to read about sports, and it was natural for Kenneth to take over the leadership. It was also natural for Marvin to take a special interest in the sports group and develop a special relationship with the boys in it, especially Kenneth. Marvin used to play ball with the boys after school, he would get excited with them about the big sports events, and he went to school games with them.

Kenneth and he really got along well. There was something like a coalition between them. Kenneth carried a lot of weight with the other kids. He took his responsibility as the sports group reading leader seriously, and, as a consequence, Marvin was able to accomplish a great deal with those boys. Marvin got to rely on Kenneth to back him up, which gave Kenneth a sense of importance. "Come on Kenneth, see what you can do about getting the kids quiet," Marvin would say. "Give me a hand, Kenneth. Help me out."

There was a free and easy feeling between the two——again, a relationship of mutual respect. Marvin and I were talking in the hall, for instance, and Kenneth walked by.

"What's happening, man?" he called to Marvin.

"I don't know, what's happening?" Marvin called back, and Kenneth walked on.

This was a boy who had regarded every teacher as an enemy.

Sometime in November an extortion incident occurred, and it looked as though everything we had accomplished would be lost. Kenneth had been taking money from one of the small boys in the class, a boy who happened to be white. There seemed to be no question about it. The dean and the boy's mother were willing to let the matter go, if I would assure them that the extortion would stop and the other boy would be protected. I was fully prepared to take that responsibility. I was by no means sure that it would not mean the end of my relationship with Kenneth.

I called him in to the office and started off indirectly. How was he getting along with the people in the class? Were there any problems? I was trying to give him an opening to tell me about it by himself. I even asked him whether he was getting along with Malcolm, who was the other boy in the case. Kenneth said nothing. Finally I came right out with it. Was he taking money from Malcolm?

He said, "So this is what this meeting is all about."

He admitted that the charge was true. We talked about what was wrong with stealing. He promised that he would not do it any more. I told him that I believed him, that I had enough faith in him to feel that he would keep his word. I would not report him; I would not call his mother. I thought enough of him to feel that once he understood what was involved, he was capable of doing the right thing without the fear of punishment.

He did keep his word. The extortion stopped. No more problems like that came up with him again. But he felt that I had tricked him, and he avoided me. I wondered how I could have handled the situation without losing his trust. As it turned out, exactly the reverse had happened. When Kenneth realized that I, in turn, had kept my word, that there had been no repercussions, and that I had trusted him to handle things himself, his relationship with me became more positive than it had before. He became more approachable, more willing to talk. On one occasion, when some high school kids were ganging up on him in his neighborhood, he was even able to admit to me that he was afraid.

The really good thing that happened with him in the Academy took place toward the end of the year. When the warm weather came around in the spring, there was a good deal of cutting class. It became clear that during one of these sorties, Kenneth and his friends had been drinking. We decided to have a group meeting to deal with it. First, I spoke to Kenneth privately to find out what had happened. Kenneth admitted that the boys had been drinking wine. Then we called the group together and got nowhere. Except for Kenneth, none of them would admit the truth.

Kenneth became angry. He told them they had to own up to what they had done. It was a struggle. The others kept denying everything, and he was getting angrier and angrier.

Finally, one of the kids said, "Hey, are you trying to get us in trouble?" I had failed to make it clear that I would not report them, if they told the truth. Before I could say it, Kenneth said it for me.

"You can tell her the truth. She's here to help you. She's not going to tell anybody what you said."

That was Kenneth as the Academy year ended. He had come to us as a hostile adolescent who saw all adults as enemies. He learned that there are people you can trust. He also gained the capacity to ask for and to receive help.

Part of the story is a postscript that has taken place since the Academy ended and is still going on as this is being written. It is now, in the year following the Academy, that the most significant changes have taken place with Kenneth. Before, we had always approached him and won his cooperation. This year he came on his own, asking for help. There had been no follow-through arrangement; we had not made a point of asking him to let us know how he was doing.

About two months after school started this year, Kenneth, now a tenth-grader in high school and a full six feet tall, appeared in the Sounding Board office. He came straight to the point.

"How are you, Kenneth?"

"Not so good."

"What's the matter?"

"I'm having trouble with my history teacher."

He had started off the same way he did with us, talking and being a wise guy in class. The teacher was a match for him. Without saying anything, he gave Kenneth a zero. "What's the zero for?" Kenneth asked. The teacher gave him another zero. Kenneth said, "Why are you giving me zeros?" The teacher gave him a third zero and a fourth. Kenneth realized that he had better be quiet.

Now the teacher taunted him. "Don't you want to talk? Is something wrong?"

From that day on the teacher had been after Kenneth without letup. Kenneth did not know how to handle the situation. Rather than explode or walk out as he would once have done, he came to us for help. The best way to deal with a teacher like that, I told him, is to fade into the background. Don't react; don't give him an excuse to ride you. Do the work and wait for the term to be over. I figured out with him how many days there were left for him in that class, and there were not many. He has followed through on my advice, and things have improved.

Kenneth has come back frequently since then. He had been staying away from school a great deal. We made a contract about it. He agreed to go in every day until March, when we would renegotiate. He was not ready to commit himself for the warm weather. So far he has kept the bargain.

125

I encouraged him to see his guidance counselor at the high school. "She's always too busy," he complained. That was undoubtedly true. I contacted her and told her about Kenneth to smooth the way. I was acting as his advocate. She promised to give him special attention—unfair to the other kids, perhaps, but a realistic recognition of the facts of life. In the giant bureaucracy of a big city high school with thousands of students, kids like Kenneth need someone to speak up for them. He started seeing the counselor, and she has been helpful to him.

Kenneth was one of the kids for whom the Academy made a big difference. In his case, while his skills did improve, the important change was in his personal development. The difference that the Academy made for Kenneth was a new perspective that opened the door on a world that had not existed for him before. I think he has a chance now of becoming part of it.

Frank

Frank is second-generation Italian, his father a skilled mechanic. Frank curses in Italian when he loses his temper, which happens often. He has been in trouble for fighting, blowing up in class, and arguing with teachers. He is a poor student, his reading level is sixth-grade. He wants to drop out of school as soon as he can. He was not known to Sounding Board before the Academy.

Frank's problem is common enough among adolescents in the lower half of schools—minimal frustration tolerance and tremendous feelings of inadequacy. He was difficult. Teachers don't know how to work with kids like Frank or how to reach them. If he found something hard to do, he would give up with an explosion, disrupting the whole class in the process. He had done poorly in school because of his "short fuse" and had been in a lot of trouble. In addition, like many teenagers, he had a problem with authority, only more so. You couldn't push him. He was extremely sensitive to any kind of authoritativeness.

At the beginning, the open structure of the Academy was an invitation to challenge. Before, it had been, "Do what I say because I'm the teacher." Now the students were being asked to speak up with no concern for the consequences. They could say what they thought, and no one would send them to the dean's office. It was an irresistible opportunity for Frank. For a time no one could finish a sentence without Frank's interrupting, until the rest of the kids complained. That was a constructive development. He was getting negative feedback from his peers, instead of from an adult.

During the first few weeks he was never far from an outburst, constantly ready to blow up. Sometimes this took an ingenious form. When Mr. Marshall insisted on keeping the windows closed at the bottom in conformance with regulations, Frank organized a strike. He got all the kids to sign a petition saying that they would do no work unless the windows were opened. There was quite a commotion about it.

When he felt that a math test had been marked unfairly, he ripped up the paper and made a big scene. He wanted another chance right then and there to show what he could do. To our dismay, the teacher decided to have a showdown. He bet Frank that he would fail to do any better and gave him another exam. From a therapeutic point of view everything was wrong with this maneuver: an adult legitimizing lack of control, the loss of face if the boy failed with the whole class watching. Fortunately, that part of it worked out well. Frank, despite his frustration intolerance, did the test and scored high.

He continued in the same pattern until well into the fall without sign of letup. Every day saw another explosion, another power struggle. When something bothered Frank, he only knew one way to handle it, and there was no reasoning with him. He objected to the work and would have nothing to do with it.

"I don't want to learn this."

"But it's important. It will help you read better."

"I don't care. I'm not going to do it."

And that was that.

To aggravate matters, he had become fast friends with four other boys whose chief interest was showing how tough they were. One way, of course, was to make trouble for the teachers and any other adult in authority. Frank's outbursts fitted right in. He was one of the boys, better than any of them at driving a teacher up the wall. The group was vehement in its scorn for learning. They were poor students, and "who cares" was the attitude they paraded in public. In addition, they were bigots. Several of them seemed to feel there was something manly about making racist remarks, and Frank was going along with them.

All of this was in the background of the group meetings with the boys and girls of Academy B that started at the end of October. At the first session of the boy's group, as my report shows, angry feelings ran high almost without restraint. As the boys got up to leave, I was concerned about how the discussion was left and discouraged by my failure to reach them. At this point, Frank turned to me and asked if we could continue the next day. That was how the group got going. The idea of continuing had not come up before.

It was the first sign of a change in Frank. The group meetings were the beginning. Then, while they were still going on, Frank got into trouble in his shop class. One afternoon, he appeared at the Sounding Board office in a state of excitement.

"Can I stay here? I have no shop to go to."

"Why not?"

"The teacher told me to get out of the class and never come back."

It was the old story. Frank had become frustrated with the work he was trying to do and had hurled his project on the floor.

We began to talk. That is when I found out that Frank's father, too, had a quick temper and exploded easily. It made things hard at home. I said I would try to help Frank not to act that way. We made an agreement, a contract. When something became too frustrating, when he first started feeling tense, he was to stop whatever he was doing. Continuing could only lead to further frustration and eventual explosion. I would let all his teachers know, so that they would not expect him to continue with something when he said that he didn't want to do it right then.

After that, if Frank was starting to go "up" in the classroom, I would try to help him to stop. I went up to him and reminded him about the agreement or asked him to come outside.

"This is what we have been talking about," I told him. "Remember you said that you don't want to explode."

Frank was finding that he could control his frustration. It apparently gave him a good feeling, a feeling of mastery over himself. He said that he did not want to go to shop or gym any more. His friends who were working left school for the afternoon. If he had a job, he would not be in these classes either. We decided to take him out of the afternoon classes. Instead, for several weeks he came to the Sounding Board office. I was fixing up the office then, and he helped me put up posters. He would climb up to the top of the bookcases and hang them for me. We would kid around because I had a terrible eye and he had to keep changing the position of the posters because I kept making mistakes. Sometimes we talked, and sometimes when he knew I was busy he would

129

just sit there. This went on for day after day while the boys' group was meeting, and our antiexplosion agreement was in full swing. The tough kid with the terrible temper was developing a trusting relationship with an adult.

It spilled over into his work. We were starting to use individual books in Academy B at about this time. That's when things really got better for Frank in the classroom. He became an enthusiastic reader. He enjoyed reading out loud to the staff, and he enjoyed reading by himself. He would sit absorbed in a book, impatient at interruptions. He used to say: "Hey, shut up, I want to read." "Wait a minute, I have to finish the chapter." "Leave me alone. I want to finish the page." What he read were popular novels: *A Stone for Danny Fisher, Harlow, The Godfather.*

As it turned out he was not able to finish *The Godfather* by June when school ended. He bought a copy of the book himself and read the rest of it over the summer. He was a boy who had never picked up a book before on his own time without somebody prodding him. He learned in the Academy what reading could be. He learned what you can get from an education, even if it is only the ability to read. He knows there are books he can read and enjoy, something he would never have known otherwise.

Once he stopped being so angry and defensive, what emerged was a tremendous amount of sensitivity and perceptiveness. At some point after the first of the year he pulled out from the tough kids and became friendly with Martin Hoffman, who was a quiet, talented boy with a dyslexia problem. I was working with Martin individually, reading with him for a period every day in the office away from the classroom. It was now spring, and it had taken a long time for Martin to be able to accept this help. Martin's development in the Academy is a story in itself.

Frank and Martin became fast friends, and Frank wanted

to join us during the reading sessions. I discouraged him, I knew how painful it was for Martin to expose his inability to read. But Frank persisted. Finally, I told him that if it was all right with Martin, he could join us. Martin was standing with us as we held this conversation. I turned to him.

"Do you want me to tell Frank why you see me?"

"I don't care," Martin answered.

I said, "Well, you tell him yourself."

Martin remained silent.

"As you can see," I said to Frank, "Martin isn't saying a word, and I'm not at liberty to tell you. You work it out with him. If it's OK with Martin, it's OK with me."

They came to me later, and Martin said it was all right for Frank to join us. I don't know what he told Frank, and I didn't ask. But Frank was obviously sensitive to Martin's problem. He brought in his own book and read by himself while I worked with Martin. When Martin mispronounced a word, Frank would look at me and then look back at his book. He was aware that something was up, and he was sensitive enough not to say anything about it. Frank's presence turned out to be a help, because it made Martin try harder. At one point, Martin rebelled against the ordeal that reading was for him. "I won't do any more. I'm not reading any more," he announced. Frank spoke to him quietly:

"Come on Martin, read. I want to read, too. Let me finish my book."

Martin came across a word he couldn't decode. It was the word "decided." He asked Frank to tell him what it was.

"No, Frank, don't tell him," I cautioned.

Martin insisted, "Come on, tell me."

Frank looked at me and looked at Martin. He didn't know what to do, because he didn't know where his loyalty lay. I was about to rescue him from the dilemma, but he moved first. He had obviously thought very quickly.

Frank said, "Well, OK. Let's break this word up. D-E is dee right?" And Martin said, "Right." "OK, and C-I-D is side?" "Right." "And E-D is ed?" And Martin said, "Right." "So what's the word?" And Martin answered, "Decided."

At the end of the year Frank and I talked about where he was and how far he had come. He knew he had made tremendous gains, he said. He wanted to keep them. We agreed that he should come and see me on a regular basis the next year. He has been keeping that commitment faithfully. Getting adjusted to high school has not been easy. But he has remained the new Frank. He is well on his way to making it.

Doris

Doris is a Puerto Rican girl from a strict home. She and her clique of Puerto Rican friends make a point of speaking Spanish together. Doris is known throughout the school for her rages and extreme behavior. She is a good math student but reads at a fourth-grade level. Last year's attempt by the Sounding Board to work with Doris in psychotherapy was a failure.

We knew about Doris' lack of control and wild fits of anger. We took her into the Academy hoping to develop a relationship with her through helping her with her skills. That would take time. Unfortunately, Doris did not give us any leeway. Almost immediately, she started to behave so outrageously that we had to take action quickly. She became angry about being in the class that she decided was for "dummies" and "crazies," and she was particularly angry at me because she thought I was responsible for keeping her there. I was the enemy.

A sample of how she acted follows, as reported by me early in October. It was a period when the regular teacher was absent, and I was handling the class with a substitute.

Doris began banging on the cabinets, and soon Nina copied her. This led to an entire class disruption, with all the kids giggling and laughing at what they were doing. I finally had to ask the two to leave, giving them a pass for the dean's office. They disappeared for a few minutes but then came back and began banging on the door. I would not allow them in. During the time they were gone, I was able to have a class discussion on their behavior. I tried to show the class that their laughing prolonged the situation. Doris and Nina continued their ferocious banging on the door.

Once a week I took over Academy A by myself for a guidance period. Doris would vie for control of the class with me, and often she was able to get it. She really made life difficult. Sometimes she would actually pull herself up and hang from the cabinets; sometimes she simply threw things around; sometimes she would run around the room or go into the closet. She misbehaved in the other classes with the rest of the staff, too, but I was her special target. She carried over the attack into the regular Academy classes, when I was there. If I walked into the classroom, she would say, "Don't you come into this room." She would make loud remarks about the clothes I was wearing. She very openly expressed a tremendous amount of hostility and was more threatening to me personally than to anyone else.

Somewhere along the line I realized that anger was only the surface symptom of Doris' operation. What was really going on was a desperate maneuver for attention. Why did she want control? Why did she want to be in charge, if not for attention? Why was she making such a big fuss about everything, if not for attention? When she would run out of the classroom, the kids would laugh, and she would get a lot of attention. She would say something nasty about me, they would laugh, and she would get attention. Everything seemed to boil down to her need for a lot of attention.

We had a case conference on her with the teachers early in October, and we agreed that, wherever possible, we would ignore her outrageous behavior. If she walked out of the classroom, we would let her go. On the other hand, whenever she behaved well, whenever she did well at her work we would praise her lavishly. She would get the attention she craved for something positive. There would be no rewards when she lost control. In other words, we were prescribing a massive dose of positive reinforcement.

Not all the teachers liked the idea. Fortunately, the two who had her in their classes were willing to go along, though we had to talk them into it. They raised the problem of what happens when other kids want to go out of the classroom too. What do you say? My answer was, You say out loud to the other kids so that Doris can hear: 'Doris and you are two different people. Doris is running out of the classroom because she wants attention, but we're not going to give her attention for things that are wrong. If she wants attention for doing things that are right, she'll get it.' If any of the other kids protest, 'you let Doris get away with everything,' the answer was, as far as I was concerned, 'your name is not Doris.' This is not a technique that teachers like to use. They don't want to make exceptions, because they are afraid of what the other kids will say.

There were three factors operating at the same time to change Doris, and they all tied in together. We were ignoring her when she lost control, and it was working. She ran out of the classroom as she had before. We let her go, and she came back. She screamed outrageous remarks, hid in the closet, banged on the cabinets, and we ignored it. Instead, we all kept repeating the same thing over and over for the whole class to hear, "Doris is only doing that because she wants attention." Doris didn't like it. Going into a tantrum had once brought her rewards, now she was suffering an unpleasant rebuff.

At the same time, whenever she behaved appropriately,

we praised her to the sky. Although her reading was poor, she was able to perform well in math, and we made a big fuss over that. Her ability, in general, was better than her performance because the explosiveness got in the way; and she could do good work in math when she wasn't angry. So while we were ignoring her disruptive behavior, we were giving her a great deal of recognition for her good work in math. She was the one, for instance, chosen to put examples on the blackboard. She glowed when she was in the limelight.

While this was going on, a real breakthrough occurred in our relationship. One day things came to a head in the group guidance class. My class was to join the other Academy group to see a film, and Doris decided that she did not want to go into the other room. As usual, the rest of the kids picked up on her lead and decided that they were not going either. Finally, with help of Susan Jaffe and every technique in the book, including threats, all of the kids went into the other classroom, except Doris. She was hiding in the closet. I closed the door. Doris came out of the closet, and we started to talk.

She was hostile, belligerent, explosive. She went up to the board and wrote, "I hate Miss Geller." Then she looked at me with fury in her eyes. "I hate you," she said.

I replied spontaneously, "Doris, sometimes I hate you too."

It was the best thing I could have done. That was the turning point. Doris' whole need was for attention and being cared about. When, for the first time, she was losing that from me, it made a big difference to her. Her fury subsided, and she calmed down. She agreed to talk things over with me at the Sounding Board office the next day.

The first thing she said when she came in was that she would talk to me but not to Mrs. Friedman or Mrs. Jaffe, because they were psychiatrists, and she "ain't crazy." I said, "If you aren't crazy, how come you sometimes act like you are?"

I reminded her of what happened the day before—how she refused to leave the room, how she hung on the cabinets and banged against the door. She had a chance to take a look at herself, and I capitalized on that. I started to imitate her tone of voice, to shriek the way she did. She began to laugh.

I said, "Doris, I'm glad you can laugh at this, because you do sound silly when you act that way. How old are you?"

"I'm fifteen."

"Do you think that's the way a fifteen-year-old should act?"

I went on: "I wish I had a tape recorder, so that I could tape it exactly and play it back to you. You'd hear how terrible you sound, and you would never want to do it again. Of course you're not crazy, but you should stop doing crazy things. You make me so mad at you. I want to like you, but when you act like that what can I do? How would you feel, if you were the teacher?"

This was the breakthrough. She saw her behavior for what it was, and she understood how I felt about it. We talked some more about the Academy—why she was in it and what she could get out of it. It was a good interaction. I told her how pleased I was that we could have this conversation, that she could talk to me at any time about anything she wanted to.

After that things got a lot better. Her behavior improved; she stopped the wild challenging; her work improved. She began to put real effort into her reading and to make genuine strides. Good reports were going out to her home, and she felt pleased about that. Her parents, of course, were delighted. They came to all the meetings, and we talked about

Doris. I discovered that they were pushing her to read more

and advised against it. "That's not the way to do it. Don't pick on her. Just don't worry about it," I told them. Afterwards, Doris asked if I had seen her parents at the meeting. I told her exactly what I had said to them. Naturally, she saw that as defending her. Our relationship became very solid.

She would come and talk with me about little problems that had come up or just to say hello. It was always done very appropriately. One problem was a big one. There was a young security guard in the school with whom the girls had been flirting. It was innocent on their part, but he didn't understand that and was making serious advances to them. One afternoon, I was in the Sounding Board office with a group of Academy boys when Doris came flying in.

"Miss Geller, I have to talk to you."

I said, "I'm busy. How about later?"

"It has to be now," she said. "In private."

She was right. It was appropriate for her to come to me at that point, and it was appropriate for her not to want to talk in front of the boys. I asked them to leave. She told me about the security guard and the advances he was making. Other girls confirmed what she said. It was reported to the principal, and the guard was fired.

She was able to transfer her positive feelings toward the whole staff. It didn't just stay with me. She used all of us. The only other problem we had with her came up in the spring when she began to cut class. She had acquired a boyfriend, and occasionally she left school with him. Whenever any student was absent, we always called their home. When we called her house, she went into a fury. There was the same old belligerence and hostility and killing looks. We decided not to call her house; she just got too angry about it. She did not cut frequently. Her gains had been too great to spoil the relationship on this issue. Instead, we handled it directly with her. "OK, Doris, we're not going to call your house. But you can't cut class. If that ever happens, you must explain to us why."

As the year progressed, her self-image got better and better. Her relationship with us grew more solid. She got a job in the afternoons in a neighborhood clothing store that was apparently very gratifying. She really felt like a big girl earning her own money. She would come in and talk about her job often. Several times, I passed by the store where she worked, and she dashed out to greet me. When her birthday came around, she talked about how she was going to celebrate it and about the new shoes she was getting for the occasion. She very much wanted to share with us. When she wore the new shoes, she sought me out to show them off.

By the end of the year the positive reinforcement program had become a memory. There was no negative behavior to ignore. There were no more tantrums. Doris still needed lots of approval and attention, but there was no need to search out opportunities for offering it. At graduation she made a great point of taking our pictures. In the fall she came to school to show them to us. They were excellent pictures, and she was delighted when we told her so. She was also pleased when I noticed that she had lost weight and complimented her on how well she looked.

Reports that have come through on Doris in high school are good. She has passed all her subjects with an average in the seventies, has had no behavior problems and a good attendance record. She is, in fact, a totally different person than she had been a year before at the start of the Academy program.

CHAPTER 9

Chronicles of Change–II

Martin

His parents came to the United States from Eastern Europe not long before Martin was born. At home they still speak their native language. In school Martin is the quiet boy who sits in the back of the room and is rarely noticed by teacher or students. His grades are among the lowest in the Academy, but he has done well in shop and art. After a few weeks, we remembered that he had not been tested.

MARTIN'S STORY was like the familiar fairy tale. The handsome prince has been bewitched and transformed into a repulsive gnome, and no one knew his true identity. Martin Hoffman had spent eight years in school labeled "stupid." From the first grade on, he had been incapable of doing the simplest kind of work. No one was very concerned, especially since Martin caused no trouble. Martin, himself, had accepted the fact a long time ago. Even some of the dumbest kids could read a little; he was unable to read at all.

He had adjusted to being stupid, and he did not care very much any more. What he did care about was being made to feel ashamed before the rest of the class. So he hid in the

139

back of the room and pretended to work while he waited for the time to pass.

But the ugly gnome, the hopeless school failure was really a handsome prince in disguise. Martin was a bright, thoughtful boy. None of his teachers knew that, because they had nothing to judge him by but his reading and written work. He never spoke in class, and they never called on him. He did not know it, because he had no other way of judging himself but by what he was able to do and by his teachers' reaction. Martin was an intelligent boy with a handicap; he had dyslexia. This is a dysfunction that makes the reading process tremendously difficult, if not impossible, unless measures are taken to deal with it.

Children with dyslexia can be taught to read. The handicap can be surmounted. Obviously, it must first be uncovered. In Martin's case, he had reached the age of fifteen and the ninth grade without any teacher becoming aware enough of him to wonder whether something was wrong. His parents, who were East European, working-class immigrants unaccustomed to question the authorities, accepted the word of the school as a matter of course. Their son was a poor student, a boy who was not very bright. Fortunately he was good with tools and did excellent cabinet work, so he would make out all right.

With the advantage of hindsight, it is easy to be critical. As it happens, we started by falling into the same trap. If we had tested him before the term began, there would have been clear warning of a problem. But Martin slipped through without being tested. He had failed to show up, a well-worn maneuver to avoid exposure, as we were to discover. For the first three weeks we hardly knew he was there. If we did notice him, it was with gratitude for at least the one student who was not acting up. Given the Academy format, however, discovery was inevitable.

140   Both of Martin's secrets came to light on the same day. I

found out that Martin was unable to read. Arlene Friedman realized that he had a fine mind. The two Academy teachers were out. We were working with the students in small groups by ourselves. It was my first contact of this kind with them in a learning situation.

I got five of the boys together and gave them a choice.

"Do you want to have a discussion about something that interests you or would you like to do some reading?"

The boys in the group included Kenneth, three of his buddies, and Martin Hoffman. Kenneth and his friends wanted to read a sports article. We agreed that each would do a paragraph out loud. As the boys started to read, Martin began acting in a way he never had before. He complained about what we were reading and got into a fight with one of the other boys.

"Who wants to read that dumb stuff? Why should they get what they want?"

He sat completely over on the side, so that he would be the last to read. Then his turn came, and I realized why. He couldn't do it. He did not know how to pronounce the simplest words; he left words out; he inserted other words; he lost his place any number of times. The rest of the boys read with considerable difficulty, but this was different. After the article was finished, I asked what they thought it meant and everyone seemed to know with the exception of Martin, who kept his mouth shut.

Earlier the same day, during the math and science period, Arlene Friedman had tried to give a group of four boys, including Martin, a chemistry lesson on acids and bases. The only one who seemed to have any interest in it was Martin. His level of comprehension, she reported, was extraordinary. He seemed completely comfortable with the presentation and was able to grasp all of the concepts. "I came away with a great deal of respect for his innate intelligence and general ability. It seems clear to me that this is a student who is being unchallenged and somehow underutilized."

Yet he could not read. Two days later I tried him out again, alone. It took a tremendous amount of reassurance and support from me before he was even able to sit down.

"Not being able to read is no crime. You'll read as well as anybody else if you work at it," I told him.

We spent an entire painful period on a single paragraph. The notion that he might be dyslexic still had not occurred to me. He was so anxious and self-conscious, I figured that this was the key to his problem.

When Arlene Friedman read with him, she was shocked. He was barely able to get through one sentence during the period. He had no grasp whatsoever of phonics or simple sight reading. He was unable to read the word "much"; he mixed up the simplest three-letter words. We agreed that he would need a great deal of individual help, but that he had the potential.

At that point we broke the students in Academy A into small groups for reading. There were about four who, like Martin, were practically not reading at all, and we put them into a group together, which I took over. Initially, all of them were reading as poorly as Martin. The others started to make progress, however, and he was staying in the same place. We realized that something more must be involved here than anxiety. It was then that we gave him a diagnostic test for perceptual functioning, and it became very clear that Martin had a problem in this area.

This was now the beginning of November. For the next two months we tried without success to convince him to cooperate with us in working on his problem. He refused to accept the idea that there was anything wrong.

He said, "You're lying. The tests are phony. You're just trying to make trouble for me."

He would not agree to have an examination at a neighborhood clinic. He would not agree to our calling his parents for permission to arrange one. Week after week all four of us on the Sounding Board staff used every argument and approach we could think of, but he would not listen. He had reconciled himself to the idea that he was stupid. He found that much less threatening.

"I don't believe that you don't understand what we're telling you," I told him once. "You're too intelligent."

"If I'm so smart," he replied, "Why can't I read?"

"Because something about the way you put together what you see has made it difficult. It does not mean that you're dumb."

"Then why didn't my teachers ever call on me, if I'm not dumb? Even when I had my hand raised."

He refused to work in class on an elementary phonics book. We made a mistake; we insisted. We were not going to coddle him and support the pretense that he was able to cope with material that was more advanced. He had to start from the beginning. What we failed to understand was the tremendous amount of pride that the boy had and the pain he suffered with exposure. He found it intolerable to work with the "babyish" book.

He began to do something that he had never done before. He became disruptive. The quiet boy who would do nothing to call attention to himself became one of the most disturbing students in the class. The armistice was off. Once we started to bother him, he started to bother us. He talked constantly and walked around the room, going from group to group and distracting the others. He was always engaging in ingenious antics that were extremely disturbing. He drew well and would sit off by himself, making sketches of people in the class that he held up for inspection. He had a trick of scraping his chair along the floor of the room and pushing

143

himself in and out around the room like a kid in a bumper car at an amusement park. He invented games and tried to get others to join him.

He spent one whole period shooting baskets through the window shades with a piece of paper. Another time he made up a game with the removable blackboard, holding it sideways and tilting a piece of chalk on it. It was a clever idea. Several of the kids could not resist getting in on it. Martin had developed into a major disruptive element in the class.

After a while we decided to have him rejoin the group of poorer readers with which I was working. The group was now reading aloud from an elementary social studies book. Usually, he refused to participate. On the few occasions when he did, he would make a tentative, halting attempt to read and then drift off or else create a disturbance in the group.

This went on for almost two months. All the while we were trying to reach him and convince him of our sincerity. We put it all down in his midyear evaluation:

Martin has consistently refused to do work in all of his subjects. His understanding and mastery of difficult material and his ability to express his thoughts in an organized way indicate that he is a very intelligent boy. All of us understand that Martin is ashamed of his inability to read. We have explained to him that just as there are different reasons why people can develop a fever, so there are different reasons why people have difficulty in learning how to read. It is perfectly true that there are people who can't read, because they are not bright enough. This is absolutely not the problem with Martin. Instead of feeling ashamed, we would like Martin to not give up on reading and to begin at the beginning.

One day in the middle of January he joined my reading group and sat next to me. I saw that he was looking at the social studies book that I was holding. I leaned over to him and whispered so that no one else could hear, "Would you like to come and read with me privately?"

He answered, "I don't care."

That always meant "yes." We agreed that he would come to the Sounding Board office during the regular English period every day. I thought it was time to compromise with our principles and adopt a more realistic approach. So far we had gotten nowhere with the phonics book. Perhaps if Martin started from the social studies book in a situation where he was protected from exposure, we might influence him to use the phonics book as well.

We started reading together at the end of January and continued through to the end of the year. Even in private, attempting to read was extremely painful to him. He refused to work with the demeaning phonics book, and I decided to give up on it. I was surprised at the amount of pride he had about reading, even when he was alone with me. A good deal of the time was spent in overcoming his resistance. He would say, "Let's talk about something. Let's not read." There was a continuous tug-of-war between us. He always said, "I don't know. I can't do it," while I insisted "Yes, you do. Yes, you can."

It was an ordeal for him. But he kept coming, and he improved. At first, it was with the greatest difficulty that he was able to get through a paragraph. By the end of the year he was reading four pages during the period. There were a variety of things that helped. He had an excellent memory and could link sounds together correctly to form a word. Many of the students were unable to do that. Then, at one point, I discovered a magazine article written by Luci Baines Johnson that related her problem with dyslexia and how she overcame it. I read it to him, and that helped. It gave him the feeling that he wasn't all that different, and his situation was not all that hopeless.

145

Our relationship became a very positive one, always with a great deal of kidding on his part. He was not yet ready to give up the defense of sarcasm. "Why don't you torture the others the way you torture me?" he would say.

He became completely serious, however, at the end-of-the-year evaluation. We met with all the students to get their reactions to the Academy. He understood what the program was about. He really grasped our philosophy. He said that the teachers cared and that he had received a great deal of help in reading, although he knew that he had a long way to go. He also said that it was hard to leave.

Martin went on to a vocational high school for students with an aptitude for crafts. We had encouraged him to apply. He should do well there, because he has a talent for working with his hands. It will depend on whether he finds adults who recognize and sustain him in his new-found identity. Martin still needs a great deal of support to believe in himself as the prince he really is.

Barbara

Barbara's family recently moved out of the ghetto area. Attractive and popular, she has many friends. Her poor academic skills are a sharp contrast to her social effectiveness. To the school, she is a major behavior problem, with a record of extensive fighting and teacher complaints. She promised to do no more fighting when we agreed to take her into the Academy.

Barbara was a pretty girl with an air of self-assurance, who was considered one of the most hostile and intractable students in the school. She was insulting to her teachers; she instigated fights. There was no way of reaching her.

"Don't be misled by her appearance," we were warned. "She's tough."

At first we were unable to understand that reputation. What we saw in her was a tremendous amount of insecurity. She read poorly and was unable to handle the simplest tasks in arithmetic. Even addition was difficult for her. The initial hostility seemed to disappear when we started to work with her in a concentrated way. She was completely cooperative. Clearly, she wanted to learn.

Then the problems emerged. This was a complex, angry girl who saw every white adult as an enemy. She would deal with you, but on her terms. Not coming too close was a basic condition of hers. How she felt and what concerned her personal life was not your business. She let us know this with brutal frankness.

One day she and her two close friends were huddled together in an animated exchange about boyfriends. My presence did not seem to be inhibiting them. Without thinking, I offered a comment. Barbara glared at me and deliberately turned her back.

"Boy, that woman's a busybody," she said in a loud voice.

During this early period we made efforts to reach her. I asked her to talk things over with me in the Sounding Board office.

"What for?"

"Something seems to be bothering you."

"I don't need you prying into my business. If anything bothers me, I can talk to my mother.

We decided to accept her terms and keep our distance. We hoped that, as the year advanced, her mistrust would lessen. She was accepting our help in reading and math. Arlene Friedman and I were working intensively with her and a few of the others who lacked elementary math skills. As her ability increased, she might come to see us differently, as people who genuinely cared. Perhaps, if that happened, the change might carry over to other adults.

147

We soon found out that we were embarking on a risky course. Barbara was perfectly willing to maintain a polite working relationship with the Academy teachers, and with us, as long as nothing occurred to offend her. Once something did, she retreated into an unshakable hostility. We saw it happen with one of her Academy teachers, and we understood what the school had been warning us about. We also understood what lay behind her anger and mistrust.

She decided that her teacher was prejudiced against blacks on the basis of some casual remarks made by him in class. The remarks were innocent; he meant nothing by them. The way Barbara heard it, he was expressing prejudice. Here was a sobering revelation of the communications gap that can undermine relations between blacks and whites. There were two incidents.

The first had to do with the championship fight between Muhammed Ali and Joe Frazier that was about to take place. This was a big event at the time; the black kids, especially, were tremendously involved with it. Someone asked Mr. Schwartz which fighter he was for.

He said, "I think boxing is a horrible sport, and I couldn't care less."

As we later learned, to Barbara that meant only one thing. Two black men were fighting each other, and he couldn't care less whether another black got killed or maimed. She never forgave him, and, despite all our attempts to reason with her later after we had developed a positive relationship, she never gave up her original conviction about it.

The second offending remark was made during a social studies discussion. The subject was the community. A heated argument developed about the safety of the ghetto neighborhood where a number of the students lived. One of them confessed that a group of black people on a corner would alarm her more than a similar group of whites.

Another countered that she was only afraid of Puerto Ricans. Interceding, Mr. Schwartz offered his experience. He said that he had once been afraid of walking in the ghetto area, but after becoming familiar with it he had lost his fears. For Barbara that confirmed his prejudices. What she heard was a statement that blacks are criminals.

From then on until the end of the year, she would have nothing to do with him. He made several attempts to explain, but it did no good. Her hostility was open and active. If he approached her, she walked away. If he spoke to her, she turned her head or even put her fingers in her ears. She made faces, snickered, muttered under her breath. Her behavior with him, it appeared, followed the pattern of her relations with teachers in the past.

Barbara's feelings about race came out into the open with explosive force in the Academy B girls' group, which held its first meeting soon after the second episode with Mr. Schwartz. Under the impact of her anger, the agenda quickly shifted from the problem of their lateness, which is what we were meeting about, to prejudice against blacks. Barbara dominated the discussion, with the other girls echoing her.

The school always presents blacks in a bad light, she stated. Teachers consider them a curiosity that needs to be "studied." She had heard prejudiced statements such as those Mr. Schwartz made many times before and they no longer hurt her. She was hardened to them. She agreed to join in further group meetings to talk about these feelings, but she saw no use in it. What she said, in essence, was that white people, and white adults especially, are bad.

While the Academy B girls were still coming together to discuss the racial issue, the sex education class got under way. Starting in November, the group met two days a week for six straight weeks into the middle of January. The relationship between Arlene Friedman, who conducted the class, and the girls in it changed perceptibly as the sessions

149

proceeded. Perhaps for the first time in their school experience they were learning something they saw as valuable.

Arlene had started out keeping the material technical and factual and steering clear of emotional issues. The girls themselves moved the discussions in the latter direction, and it was Barbara who led the way. The element of an intimate exchange was now added to the scientific approach with which Arlene Friedman had started. She wrote in one of her reports:

The conversation turned to boyfriends and premarital sex, and we talked about forced marriages. This led to a discussion about the different rates at which boys and girls mature. The girls had a lot to say about this. I pointed out that most boys matured later and slower than girls did. They were not really ready for a relationship where they considered the needs of the girl, cared about her, and respected her until they were seventeen or eighteen at the earliest. I suggested that this is one reason most girls do not become sexually involved with boys until they are older. They don't have the rest of the relationship to go with it. I pointed out that without a good relationship, sex was not very meaningful.

The sex education class became centered more and more around discussions like that, with Barbara one of the most active and open participants. She did not seem to consider Mrs. Friedman a "busybody." It was probably the first time that she had dropped her guard with a white adult, the enemy.

For the first time, too, she was learning math. It was a hard, tedious process. Both Barbara and her two friends, who were together in the slowest math group, had to start almost from the beginning. They had never become proficient in addition; they were unable to do subtraction. One problem in working with them was their embarrassment at the elementary level of the work they were doing. If any of the other students came over, they covered up their papers and refused to work until the intruders went away.

With Barbara there was another problem that blocked her progress. She was afraid. This feeling went beyond a fear of failing. She seemed paralyzed by the conviction that she couldn't do it. Underneath the facade of sophistication and social knowhow, there was a devastating feeling of inferiority. For long periods she would sit immobilized, unable to focus on the work before her. Little by little her confidence grew, as she found that the tasks were simple enough to be possible for her and that she could risk saying "I don't know" without disapproval.

Finally, she made a real breakthrough. For a long time she had been struggling with the mechanics of borrowing in subtraction. One day she found that she could do it. The effect was electrifying. Her face lit up. She was unable to contain her excitement. She asked if she could show her work to the Academy teachers, so they "won't think I'm stupid." She ran around the room displaying what she had done to the other students. There was a tremendous sense of identification with learning something and proving that she was not "dumb." It was poignantly apparent how important this was to her.

After that she moved ahead rapidly. Now she had a feeling that she could do it, and she was willing to work very hard. She came to the Sounding Board office for extra instruction in the afternoon. She went on to simple division and by the end of the year had mastered long division. Her pride in these accomplishments was enormous. She took to bringing her work home to show her mother what she was doing.

Her relations with us when we were teaching her became warm and relaxed. She and the other girls would tease us in a friendly way. Once, when they wanted to take a breather, they announced with big grins that they had serious emotional problems to discuss. Another day Barbara was having difficulty with a new operation in division and attempted some delaying maneuvers. It was the familiar routine of wanting a drink of water and asking for a bathroom pass. In the middle of this she smiled at me and said, "You know, I'm trying to get out of the situation."

She talked gratefully about the help she was getting. "I'm learning a great deal and I want to thank you," she told me at one point in the late spring.

When a visitor asked what she thought of the program, she said, "If it weren't for Mrs. Jaffe and Mrs. Friedman I would know nothing in math. They've really helped me."

The most dramatic change occurred in her willingness to confide in us. After the sex education classes and the breakthrough in her work, she no longer felt that her personal concerns were not our business. Many intimate group conversations took place in an informal way with her and her friends, and she sought us out privately.

One day she asked if we could talk alone. What should "someone" do, she asked, if she wanted to be friendly with a crowd of girls who rebuffed her overtures? Another time, she drew me aside to ask my advice about a problem a "friend" was having with an unfaithful boyfriend.

Positive relationships had developed between Barbara and the Sounding Board staff, but we wondered whether it would carry over to other adults. Things had not worked that way with Mr. Schwartz. Close as she was to us, she never relented in her hostility toward him. One year and a few relationships seem hardly enough to transform a fifteen-year pattern. Something has happened since Barbara went on to high school, however, that indicates that the Academy experience may have had a real impact.

Barbara went on to a secretarial high school. She had made great advances in her skills, but they were still not good enough for the demands being made. She was having a hard time in math. In the early fall we received a call from the guidance counselor in her school. Barbara had come to her for help. Once that would have been inconceivable. Evidently, she had come to feel that adults can be trusted.

It would be pleasant to leave Barbara's story on that optimistic note. But the facts need to be stated. Barbara's new-found attitude may not survive long in the face of reality. In the case of adolescents from Barbara's world, adults are indeed not always to be trusted; they do not always care. The guidance counselor who contacted us was calling to complain about the persistent girl demanding her time! She thought there might be something wrong about her. How do you explain to a vulnerable adolescent that adults—but only some of them—honestly want to help.

Richard

He was a young, black, fifteen-year-old from a large ghetto family. The oldest brother was the good one who did things right; Richard was the one who got into trouble. Ever since he entered first grade the only reports coming home about him had been complaints about his behavior or poor work. He was considered incorrigible and would have been in one of the special schools for discipline problems, if not for overcrowding.

The year before Richard had been one of our major failures. After months of seeing him on a weekly basis, we had given up. He seemed impossible to reach. He had referred himself, but not with anything therapeutic in mind. He was accused of vandalizing a bus, was afraid that he would be sent to court, and had been told by his friends that the Sounding Board could help him.

"I think trouble follows me," he said that first time.

"Would you like to stay out of trouble?"

"Sure."

Outside of something serious like a court hearing, however, trouble did not really bother him. He was failing four subjects and was slated for a disciplinary school because of truancy and disruptive behavior. Yet everything was "I don't care." There was no reason to change.

"Don't you want to do well in school?"

"What for?"

He was frank, good-humored, and deaf to what we were trying to communicate.

"Richard, don't you understand that if you could only be quiet in class, you wouldn't get all these referrals to the dean?"

"So, let them give me referrals. What do I care?"

He was constantly in trouble for wandering around the halls and creating a disturbance while classes were in session.

"Why do you act that way? You're just asking for trouble."

"Listen, the only reason I come to school is to have fun and fool around. Otherwise, I might as well stay home."

Only once did a crack appear in his armor. That was when Susan Jaffe, who was working with him, asked to see a math test he had failed. He tried to avoid showing it to her. When she went over it with him, he lost his nonchalance and became visibly agitated. She could see that he barely understood the simple multiplication operation that was involved. She offered to help him learn how to do it and assigned him some problems as a start. He never did them.

In the Academy Richard carried on in the old way only for a short time. The change came with a swiftness and thoroughness for which we were unprepared. It was nothing less than a transformation, and it happened one day several weeks after the start of the term. We were now split into small groups both in reading and math. Richard was in the slowest group for both subjects. Not until we were with him in the classroom did we realize how poor were his academic skills. He was almost a nonreader. He had not mastered the basic operations in arithmetic. It was small wonder that he avoided working, for he was not able to work.

On this day in the middle of October, I was with the slow math group. The assignment was to do some pages in the workbook. Richard, as usual, was not working. I went over to him, sat down, and went through a problem with him. Then I watched while he did the next one by himself. He got it right. It was an achievement.

"Richard, I'm proud of you. You did that beautifully, try the next one."

He gave me a pleased look and kept going. Throughout the period I kept going over and showering him with attention. Every time he got a problem right, I praised him. He did a whole page, and then he did another whole page, working with furious concentration.

At the end of the math period, Dr. Holmes, the Sounding Board director, came into the room. I called out to her in front of the group.

"You should see what a magnificent job Richard did. You wouldn't believe that one person could cover so many problems and get them right."

She shook his hand. "Richard, that's great," she said.

Janet Geller came in at this point to work with the slow readers' group in social studies. Dr. Holmes turned to her.

"Wait till I tell you what Mrs. Friedman said about Richard today. He broke the bank in math. He really did a fantastic job."

The reading group formed, and Dr. Holmes sat next to Richard. Before this, he had refused to read out loud, except for one painful attempt during which the other kids laughed   155 at him. Now, with Dr. Holmes virtually holding his hand, he struggled through a whole paragraph sounding out every word. After the reading session, they all called me into the room. Richard's face was shining as I had not seen it before.

"You must hear what Richard was able to do. If he keeps this up he will really be reading."

From that day on, there was nothing Richard would not do for the Sounding Board staff. He gave up his refusal to work completely. Now he went to the other extreme. It was as though a dam had burst. No more coming in late, no more fooling around, no more avoiding contact with us. In the math group, when he was finished with an assignment, he asked for more. In the reading group, he was the first to volunteer and clamored for extra chances. He asked us to read with him in class and during the passing time between periods. He came to our office for special help, giving up precious gym periods and lunch periods. At the slightest praise and approval he became like a child at Christmas.

In one of my daily reports during this period, I wrote: "Richard has changed from being Public Enemy Number Three to a sheer delight in the classroom."

The improvement in his reading was dramatic. In a few short weeks he had advanced to the point where he could go through a lengthy passage at a reasonable rate without making mistakes. He was able to sound out complicated words that a short while before would have been totally beyond his capacity. His comprehension left a great deal to be desired, but he had taken the first step to becoming a reader, something that had not happened in eight years of school. He had improved so much that we decided to have him act as the leader of his reading group.

We sent letters and reports home letting his parents know how well he was doing. It took some convincing.

"My mother said I must have changed my report card, because it was so good," he said to me. But he was beaming.

His father and mother attended the first parents' meeting, and we told them how great their son was.

"He's our star pupil."

They looked skeptical, and he squirmed uncomfortably. At the next meeting we again told them what outstanding progress Richard was making. This time his mother gave him a big hug. His success had begun to make a difference in the way his parents felt about him. He was winning approval at home, too.

He was desperate for it. If there were one word I would use to describe Richard, it is "hungry." There was a powerful, primitive need in him for emotional feeding, a need that apparently had not been adequately met by an adult before. His disruptive behavior had served this need in two ways. It had been a device to win substitute approval from his peers and had acted as a smokescreen to conceal the fact that he had no academic skills and to protect him from the shattering disapproval that discovery would bring. In the Academy the smokescreen was no longer necessary.

With the transformation came new problems. Now that he was at last receiving approval and praise, Richard was insatiable. He wanted our exclusive attention. He seemed to need unlimited support. In the reading group he was hogging the show. When he could not dominate it, he became difficult. The boy who had refused to participate and could not be induced to read out loud wanted no one else to share the spotlight with him. When another student was reading, Richard would talk to the person beside him or interrupt to correct mistakes that were being made.

I called him into the Sounding Board office to talk about his behavior during the reading group. We spoke about how well he was doing in his reading but pointed out that he had to cooperate and give others a chance. Reaching him with this concept was difficult. Richard was a youngster operating at an egocentric level who had not yet reached the stage of being concerned with anyone but himself. He should be allowed to read, he said, because he had caught on to reading.

"What about the other kids? How are they going to learn if you give them the answers?"

"I'm only trying to help them."

With a great deal of explanation and help from me, Richard was able to say that other kids deserved as much of a chance as he did. He was probably only saying it to please me.

Our success with him had opened up a serious dilemma that was built into the Academy operation. How much attention could we give one child when so many others were also hungry? Yet how could we hold back the support that was the oxygen that had brought him to life and enabled him to function. Hopefully, as time went by and he grew more sure of himself he would need less and less of it. Right now, like a dependent infant, his growth seemed to depend on our nurturance. In the meanwhile, other kids were telling us in so many words that they wanted attention, too.

Limited resources and limitless needs are a familiar problem in the helping professions. But we were encountering it now in a new guise. As therapists operating in the conventional appointment system, we had been forced to restrict the number of our clients in line with available time and personnel. Once a commitment was made, however, the youngster who was our client was assured of our total involvement and concern within the period assigned for treatment. In the Academy all of the students were our clients and all of their needs were pressing on us at once. We found ourselves groping for a new concept of our responsibility. The old one was not much use in this situation.

Richard posed the dilemma in an acute form. Unfortunately, we were never to resolve it in his case, because an
unexpected turn of fate took the matter out of our hands. At

the end of January Richard's father was killed in an automobile accident. In the aftermath, Richard went through a period of withdrawal from school—both physically and psychologically. We were left with many unanswered questions. About one point, however, we could be sure. Whatever further progress might have been cut off, it became apparent that we had built a relationship with Richard that stood on firm ground.

After his father's death Richard stayed home for almost a month. He sent us a message through a friend.

"Richard asked me to tell you that he's not coming to school, because his father died."

He clearly cared enough about our good opinion to be disturbed that we might think he had turned truant again.

When he returned to school, he came straight to the Sounding Board office. He did not want to talk about his father or discuss his feelings. He wanted to establish contact, and he wanted our help.

He said, "Please help me stay in school, because I really don't want to be here now. I really find it hard to be in school."

We tried, but it was difficult. He had no phone, so that we were unable to call him as we usually did when kids were absent. He was in one day, out one day for a long while. When he returned to school after staying out, we always told him, "Remember, Richard, you said that you wanted us to help you stay in school."

It was not until May that he started to come in regularly. But he was late every single day both in the morning and after lunch. The school placed him on the excessive lateness list, which meant that he would fail to receive a diploma unless he reformed quickly.

We made an agreement that committed him to be on time every day. It was a contract. To help him keep it, we drew up a weekly chart and hung it in the Sounding Board office. *159*

When he was on time, the chart was marked with a check. If not, the word "late" was written in. At first he continued being late, but soon it obviously came to matter that he should keep his contract. One morning he walked into the office, took a pencil, strode over to the chart, and dramatically marked himself in on time. After that—it was now close to the end of the year—he came in on time every day.

We will never know how Richard might have developed if his year had not been disrupted. As it is, he remains our "star pupil" with remarkable academic gains that were accompanied by a simultaneous transformation in his behavior and self-image. We liked to say in the Academy that good learning is good therapy. Richard was an excellent example of that.

CHAPTER 10 *What the Sounding Board Learned*

THE THERAPEUTIC CLASSROOM model we started with was to be a first step, the takeoff point for an open-ended experiment. From the Academy classes we would learn where the idea could lead. Up to now we have reported on developments that followed from our original expectations and formulation. But there were also developments we had failed to anticipate, most often in the nature of unexpected difficulties and problems.

The students were not the only ones who underwent a learning experience. We did, too. Only when theory was translated into day-to-day practice did issues come in focus that were clearly crucial to the kind of innovation we were attempting. These issues had to do with the students, the teachers, and the school milieu. Not unlike babes in the woods, we were surrounded by unanticipated perils and pitfalls.

Of course, we should have been aware. In retrospect, we can only marvel at the naiveté with which we embarked on what amounted to a cultural revolution in a social institution still very much intact. The fact is that for all the talk of crisis and change in urban education, traditional attitudes, values, and power relationships still hold sway in the public schools, if Kennedy Junior High is an indication. Unfortunately, the Academy program was launched in such haste—in itself typical of the school's operation—that questions of this kind had to be shoved aside during the brief planning and preparation period.

However, given the same handicaps and limiting circumstances, we would still make the same decision to go ahead. Winning professional laurels for a flawless experiment was not our ambition. What we were seeking was a way to help children who had immediate needs. The opportunity to test the therapeutic classroom in a carefully controlled experimental setting might have been a long time coming; it might never have come at all.

As it turned out, by trying it in a normal, if not adverse, school setting, we were avoiding the trap that has tripped up innovations developed under "clean" laboratory conditions. Many of the most promising programs fail because they cannot withstand the harsh test of real life in the public schools. In our case, problems that a more protected environment would undoubtedly have obscured were forced into the open. The key lessons they brought home centered around three themes:

1. *Stigma*—We learned that student shame at being labeled in a remedial program can seriously weaken its effectiveness.

2. *Overadjusted teachers*—We learned that the teacher

whose professional identity is bound up with the traditional system will have difficulty switching to a therapeutic approach, even if he favors it.

3. *School priorities*—We learned that differences in priorities and values are likely to produce an atmosphere of mistrust when an innovation such as the therapeutic classroom is attempted in a conventional school.

Lesson #1—Stigma

Experts say that disadvantaged adolescents place a low value on academic achievement. That may be true. Nevertheless, it is also true that the feeling of being stupid fills them with a desperate sense of shame and that for most of them a remedial program represents public exposure and disgrace. Anyone who thinks that nonlearners are indifferent to failure in school should see, as we did, their anxiety at taking tests, their resistance to "babyish" tasks, and their concern about grades. They care intensely. Anyone who discounts the significance of school failure for an adolescent's status among his peers should try to reason, as we did, with a fifteen-year-old who has been taunted about being in a class for "retards."

One of the first things we learned was that we had underestimated the stigma factor as a threat to what we were trying to do. The countermeasures we had taken hardly began to touch it. We had named the program the Academy to suggest selectivity and to circumvent the demeaning numbering system that broadcasts a group's ability level. With a few calculated exceptions, we had limited the classes to students who voluntarily chose to be in them and who made an explicit commitment to our goals. In their own words they wanted to improve their reading, and they wanted to be in a special class designed for that purpose.   *163*

Furthermore, we were providing them with an accepting and unregimented school environment geared to their authentic interests and needs.

We took it for granted that the Academy students would be delighted with their liberation from authoritarian restrictions and meaningless tasks. We expected them to welcome the flexibility and personal emphasis of an informal classroom. We thought that the rewards of real learning plus an understanding of the stakes involved would more than counteract the embarrassment of working with elementary material. In the long run we were right, but we miscalculated on two scores and ran into unforeseen difficulties as a result.

Shame is a painful and powerful emotion that works on several levels and in subtle ways, of which public exposure is only one aspect. Equally distressing is the inner humiliation that comes with seeing oneself as deficient and carrying the secret knowledge of a "spoiled identity," to use the phrase of Erving Goffman. We are all familiar with the strategies of concealment that people (ourselves included) use to protect themselves against the devastating moment of truth. When there is no other recourse, pretense and self-deception become psychological necessities. As Eugene O'Neill argues in *The Iceman Cometh*, life seems to be impossible without illusions.

The Academy program subjected the students to double jeopardy with respect to stigma. Like a scarlet letter, it fixed a visible label on them and, in addition, threatened to strip away their private defenses. Their reaction was instantaneous. In the first weeks we were hearing constant complaints about being in a class for "dummies" and bombarded with requests for transfer. Of more direct consequence to the conduct of the program, we were getting resistance to its form and content. What it came down to was that the students needed *not* to be different. In eliminating the familiar system in terms of which they had fabricated their defenses, we had removed the props of their pretense.

They wanted to be like the other ninth graders. They wanted the regular curriculum. They wanted homework. They wanted to learn algebra, not multiplication tables like fourth graders. They fought against small group instruction, uneasy without the passive anonymity of a large class. They fought against reading aloud like "babies." They fought against the phonics system, for which we had such high hopes, with such intensity that we abandoned it after less than a month. More surprising and revealing, they objected to our being "too nice." They felt they were receiving special privileges as though there were something wrong with them, as though they were not normal.

As the Academy classes began to provide increasing rewards, these attitudes changed, rapidly for some students, more slowly for others. The need for the old defenses lost its urgency, and the grip of shame relaxed, to be replaced by growing feelings of self-approval. Within the Academy, at least, stigma lost its devastating impact for all but a few. The resistance to "babyish" work and unfamiliar procedures weakened.

A combination of events operated to bring this process about. Our reinforcement and encouragement encouraged a positive self-image. The development of trusting relationships provided support. Most crucially, there was the unexpected, unknown, and intensely gratifying experience of mastery as skills increased.

The very nature of the process, however, demanded time. Our mistake had been to plunge in abruptly without allowing for an adjustment period before learning a different way of working. Even more important, the students needed such preparation in order to be armored against the blow of public exposure.

165

If they had been insulated from school pressures, the stigma factor would undoubtedly have been less significant, especially after the rewards of the Academy took over. Unfortunately, through the year there continued to ge outside incidents that rubbed salt in the wound and kept the issue alive. The depth of the problem can be seen from Janet Geller's account of an episode and its aftermath. Miss Geller reported it in the daily record. It occurred in January, when the program in Academy A was well launched and strong relationships had been established between our staff and the students involved.

A situation occurred today in auditorium that upset many of the kids, particularly Kenneth Mansfield. New seats were being assigned, and when the teacher in charge called for Academy A, nobody moved. Apparently he called them a second time, and still no one moved. At that point some of the other kids began to call Academy A "dummies." At the same time, the teacher told them to get moving in an irritable way. When the class came back, a lot of the kids complained that everybody said they were "dummies."

Kenneth was especially upset. He and several of his buddies refused to come into the classroom and insisted that they wanted to get out of the Academy. We finally got everybody back in the room and had a group discussion about what had happened in the auditorium. The kids were furious. Doris, in particular, challenged me, saying that when her friend wanted to join the Academy I had said that she was too smart for the class. I tried to correct the misconception, pointing out that it was a matter of reading scores and not of being smart, which were two different things. The reason people were in the class was because of their low reading scores, and Doris' friend had a reading score that was too high for us. However, Doris continued to be slightly hysterical and make wild accusations. She was followed in this by Sylvia and John.

I found that the best technique was to go over to each person who was being hysterical, put my hands on them, and talk with them individually, regardless of whether I had to repeat myself. I managed to get everyone calmed down, except for Doris and John. John, who is usually very reasonable, was only partially convinced of what I was saying and told me that he wanted to get out of the

Academy, too. Kenneth was threatening to strike tomorrow. The class ended on this note.

By the next day the excitement was forgotten or at least neutralized as a result of our strenuous efforts to work things through, as well as by the positive pull of the experiences they were having in the class. In the last analysis, the most potent element was the credit we had established. Most of these students by now had an investment in their relationship with us, and we drew on it heavily. In this case, where matters were almost out of control, we resorted to the extraordinary tactic of telephoning Kenneth Mansfield at home. The daily report ends:

I spoke to Kenneth in the afternoon, but he was unyielding, still presenting arguments as to why he should get out of the class and insisting that Academy A would strike tomorrow. That was the situation when we left. Since Kenneth was the leader of the strike, and no strike would take place without him, I thought it might be worthwhile for Dr. Holmes to make a direct appeal to him at home before matters went any further. She phoned him in the evening, and he was extremely impressed that "Dr. Holmes" was calling him. She was able to reason with him as to why it was appropriate for him to be in the class, why the kids in the class were not dumb, and why the class was of benefit to him. Kenneth agreed to everything. At the end of the conversation, Dr. Holmes asked him about the strike, and he assured her there would be no strike tomorrow. I'm sure the situation has been salvaged.

Could it have been avoided? Even with the advantage of hindsight, we are not sure. It may be that the labeling problem presents a built-in dilemma that must be faced as an intrinsic aspect of any remedial program such as the therapeutic classroom when it operates in a traditional context. At this point, a number of countermeasures seem promising. Whether or not any of them make a difference, and how much of a difference, only a trial run will tell.

One possibility would be to minimize contacts between

students in the program and the rest of the school. Another would be a preliminary orientation period before the program starts to build up an *esprit de corps* and heighten motivation, thereby providing some protective immunization against stigma. Then again, if the program were started when students first entered the school, and before they have internalized its values, it should find them at a less vulnerable stage. For this reason, we had originally wanted to conduct the Academy with a seventh-grade group. We also had hoped thereby to sensitize the entire faculty and encourage their aid. Sad to say, at Kennedy Junior High some of the most harm was done by teachers who seemed oblivious to the students' feelings.

Lesson #2—Overadjusted Teachers

All four of the Academy teachers had responded enthusiastically to the therapeutic classroom idea as first presented to them. They were eager to take part in an innovation to reverse educational failure, even though it would call for radical departures from established practices. Or so they said, and we had no reason to doubt their sincerity at the time. During those meetings in the late spring of the preceding term, there seemed to be a happy meeting of minds on essentials. True, our unorthodox approach to curriculum aroused some concern, and so did the division of roles in the classroom. But they were ready to wait and see. Everyone understood that this was a venture that necessarily involved uncertainty. There was no fixed script to guide us. We would have to play it by ear.

What none of us realized was the extent of the readjustment the therapeutic classroom would demand of the teachers. It called for a switch in thinking at a fundamental level, an abandonment of the old securities that supported their professional identity. Of the four teachers, three were unable to make the transition.

Despite good intentions, it was impossible for these teachers to shift from authoritarian discipline, structured front-of-the-room teaching or a prepackaged course of study. Working things through on a trial-and-error basis, with its inherent and inevitable frustrations, left them with tremendous anxiety. Most especially, this problem applied to spelling out lines of authority between teaching and Sounding Board roles, a process that underwent a continuing process of redefinition as the program evolved. They needed to know who was the ultimate "boss."

In the traditional classroom, by traditional criteria, these three were excellent teachers who controlled their classes, covered the prescribed curriculum, and ended up liked and respected by the students and colleagues. Within the context of the Academy, they were unable to function. They were, in fact, failures, who left the program with a sense of dissatisfaction and defeat. The fourth teacher, on the other hand, was a promising novice who had come into the classroom only the year before, directly after college, and was still finding his way professionally. Teaching might be a temporary way-station for him or a permanent career. He neither felt a commitment to it, nor did he have a professional identity to protect. "I don't think of myself as a teacher," he said at one point.

After a few false starts he had made the switch, becoming adept at handling small groups, working out curriculum materials, and dealing with students in terms of their personal dynamics. With him we were able to develop an easy, give-and-take relationship without the intrusion of authority questions. He ended the year a convert to the therapeutic approach and eager to try it again.

The lesson goes beyond the general proposition that successful adjustment to an established role makes change   *169* difficult. The critical issue is what successful adjustment has entailed; what degree of independence, flexibility, autonomy it permits; what kind of personal orientation it requires. To understand that, the outcome must be examined within the framework of the system to which the accommodation has been made.

Discussing teacher participation in educational change, Sarason (1971) declares, "The first two years of teaching are a baptism of fire in which many things can be consumed, including some of the ingredients that make for a good and even outstanding teacher. The important point is that what happens in these years, *for good or for bad*, cannot be understood by narrowly focussing on the teacher, but by seeing the teacher as part of a matrix of existing relationships, practices, and ideas" (p. 171).

During the Academy year at Kennedy Junior High we had front row seats for the system in operation as it shaped the individuals within it into a constraining mold. Situated inside the classroom, we could see why teachers behave the way they do. We could also see why so many leave the profession, get tuned out, and abandon their original idealism. As mental health professionals, we were in a protected position. The court of judgment significant for our self-image was located in another world, one to which we could always return. Still, the pressures of the school system as they operated in Kennedy Junior High frequently came too close for comfort, or close enough to make painfully clear what adjustment to the system meant.

The year before, working as a separate unit in the school, we had found it shocking that teachers should place order above learning and show reluctance to extend themselves beyond the minimum requirements of their jobs. Their attitudes seemed more appropriate for workers on an assembly line than for responsible adults entrusted with the shaping of young lives. With our new vantage point came a new comprehension of how these attitudes are generated. After one especially revealing experience, Arlene Friedman put her reactions into words. Several days before, she had been left alone with Academy A for the first time. The memo she wrote was an attempt to analyze what had happened. She called it "The Plight of the Teacher—What Is and What Is Not Possible in the Public Schools."

Since working in Kennedy Junior High, we have often looked with dismay at the professional level of teachers in the public school system. We have noted with disapproval their unwillingness to meet for workshops or any kind of learning experience, their tendency to put in the minimum amount of effort, saving free periods and prep periods for games of ping-pong and pinnochle, and the contemptuous way they are known to refer to their students. As mental health professionals, we have decried this lack of concern and humanity. We have also attempted to offer alternatives to it, but the one thing that we have not done successfully is to understand it.

After one day last week, I began to understand, and I want to share this insight with the rest of the staff. For me the day began with the unexpected news that there were no teachers available for Academy A, and I would have to handle the class by myself for both math and social studies. The four periods that followed were one interminable nightmare, which I will not attempt to describe in all their harrowing details.

In brief, for whatever reason, the kids were completely out of my control, especially the boys. They hid behind the blackboard, they punched each other, they shouted and complained, and they ran all over the room. In an attempt to be "teachery" I made a number of dire threats about demerits, dean's office, and the like. I also screamed, cajoled, and pleaded. All to no avail.

At one point, several of the boys ran into the halls yelling, and then proceeded to punch, kick, and chase each other with the enthusiasm of Cassius Clay, Roger Bannister, and the Rockettes. A teacher with whom I was unfamiliar passed by and on seeing them in the hall began to mutter in my direction about how these students should be sent to the dean's office and their behavior was outrageous. At that moment, I completely agreed with her.

I could discuss the therapeutic implications of these four

171

periods or describe the dynamics of the students involved, but the point of this memo is, instead, to give you the therapeutic and dynamic considerations from my point of view. I felt destroyed. I felt that I had been effectively steamrollered and that I had no control over the situation. Most important, I was extremely glad that I did not have to face them the next day. I did not like the students. I did not like their behavior, but I also did not like them.

I did not like myself. I felt like a failure, inadequate and incompetent. The devastation was made more dreadful by the fact that I felt I did not want anyone to know how badly things had gone.

I spent the rest of the day in a purple funk, muttering and cursing under my breath. I did not see any students for tutoring, for counseling, or any other purpose. If I had been enrolled in a workshop program, I would have cut. If there were somebody to play ping-pong with, I think I would have. For the first time, I understood how completely and totally overwhelming the job of classroom teacher can be. For the first time I, too, would not give up my lunch, prep, or free periods to work with a group of individual students.

After a few days away from Kennedy Junior High, my sense of perspective returned. I began to look at teachers in classrooms in a a new light. I began to understand the compromises the classroom teacher must make.

Confronted with thirty-five faces, there is little that one can do except strike for the middle, knowing that at least 30 and more likely 50 percent of the students will be lost; and one must train oneself not to care. If one stops to pick up the stragglers, the result is always chaos. And chaos has a high cost in morale for the classroom teacher.

I began to understand the use of power. Therapists obtain power through a relationship. The teacher does not have this available to him and, therefore, he obtains power by trading on other people's power, namely deans with their suspensions and disciplinary procedures. It is unfair, it is nontherapeutic, but it is, unfortunately, necessary.

I began to understand, too, the lack of compassion, the lack of humanity that teachers seem to project in discussing their students. If one bleeds and cries for every lost soul, there will be no time to reach anyone given a classroom of thirty students. If one really takes teaching seriously, the result is paralysis, the inability to teach. I find this a horrifying conclusion, but I feel very strongly that it is so.

What is the answer? I think I know. The answer is the Academy, classes of twenty students with two professionals in the room. The answer is not necessarily a question of therapy but management of what is and is not possible.

The teacher who is successful in the traditional public school system has to be, or become, a person who can accept severe limitations on his freedom of action. The built-in constraints of conventional classroom organization, which Arlene Friedman experienced, is only one. There is very little in the teacher's position, as it has developed in the public schools, that permits the kind of autonomous performance usually associated with professional occupation. Teachers have become, as Brenton (1970), has said, like "mass production workers on an educational assembly line" (p. 109).

What the Sounding Board learned through first-hand encounter with the realities of school life has been reported time and again by objective observers of public education. The rank-and-file teacher occupies a lowly status at the bottom of bureaucratic hierarchy, hedged in by restrictive rules that touch on the most fundamental aspects of his job. Not only does he have no need to make basic decisions about his work, he lacks the power to do so. Policy matters are out of his hands.

Subject to constant supervision and evaluation, he is told what to teach, when to teach, how to teach, and what materials to use. In many schools, including Kennedy Junior High, he is expected to submit lesson plans, accept official assignments, and follow a rigid daily time schedule. Perhaps the most important criterion by which he is judged is his ability to maintain an orderly class.

The situation is hardly conducive to spontaneity or innovative thinking. On the contrary, the rewards of the   *173* system go to the teacher who, like the good soldier, can follow orders. Above all, he covers the prescribed curriculum in the allotted time with the assigned textbooks, whether or not the students have learned anything, and he conducts a class where students sit quietly at their desks, at least whenever a supervisor enters the room. Both of these achievements call for special skills that automatically preclude any one-to-one relationships. The successful public school teacher, both by training and practical necessity, is group-oriented.

Exceptional individuals have sometimes broken through the constraining mold either by subterfuge or sheer force of personality. Exceptional supervisors have sometimes made it possible for creative teachers to evade the tentacles of the system. By and large, however, and despite a seemingly endless parade of educational reforms, the pressures on the public school teacher remain the same, and the "successful" teacher is the one who can adjust to them. Those for whom the interferences and constraints are intolerable soon drop out, as the attrition rate among teachers testifies.

Small wonder that the three veteran teachers at the Academy found it difficult to function in a therapeutic classroom setting. Such a setting called for qualities and capacities they had suppressed too effectively. Their adjustment to the system had been too complete. They were trapped in the mold. As far as a therapeutic classroom program is concerned, the lesson we learned about overadjusted teachers indicates the need for careful screening in the selection of teachers. The lesson does not mean that only the neophyte will find it possible to work in the new way, although the beginning teacher may well be the most likely prospect. With an explicit exchange of views beforehand and a thorough preparation for the switch in philosophy and method that is involved, we are convinced that many experienced teachers who have stayed on and made their peace with the system will find the therapeutic classroom an exciting and welcome opportunity to give up the compromises and become the kind of teacher they had once hoped to be.

Lesson #3—School Priorities

Before the Academy, early in 1970, the administration of Kennedy Junior High undertook an "innovation" on its own initiative, a rare event. The small, self-contained class conducted by Linda Melnick had proved successful in modifying the disruptive behavior of some outstanding troublemakers. Now the school decided to set up its own self-contained unit in hopes of achieving the same result. What it did was to copy the form of what we were doing, while completely ignoring questions of content and procedures.

In short order, fifteen of the "worst" ninth-grade boys were put together in a room with a muscular male teacher unacquainted with therapeutic thinking or techniques. There he was left to flounder on his own, with neither guidance nor supervision. The outcome was a disaster. Five of the fifteen immediately became truants. Most of the others refused to stay in the room and took to roaming the halls and creating a disturbance. The school soon decided that the project was a ghastly mistake and gave it up, confirmed in a deeply entrenched distaste for change.

The brief and unhappy history of class 9–13, as this self-contained unit was called, gives some hint of the climate in which the Academy program was conducted and the problems connected with it. The school was dominated by conventional thinking and motivated by expediency in its approach to innovation. Fundamental differences in priorities, values, and time perspective separated the

Sounding Board and the administration. On our part they called for a fine balance between accommodation and firmness, which put our diplomatic skills and capacity for tolerance to the test. It was not easy.

If the Academy had been launched under protected conditions, we might never have learned the hard facts of life about attempting change in a school committed to the status quo and a pervasive "no-wave" philosophy. At Kennedy Junior High we were working in an atmosphere of mistrust and constant obstruction. The success of the program *in spite of* these difficulties is, we think, one of the best proofs of its validity.

One point must be underlined. Our experience has been limited to one school. In all fairness, we have no right to generalize beyond it. The winds of change are said to be blowing strong in American education. Conceivably, although we strongly doubt it, Kennedy Junior High is "one of a kind," and the opposition and lack of sympathy we encountered there unique. Given that the school is enmeshed in a giant bureaucracy that has long imposed uniformity on its component units, and given the evidence of authors like Charles Silberman, we are more inclined to believe that it is still typical of schools in large city systems. Nevertheless, what we have to say here is necessarily limited to our own experience.

Our troubles came from two sources and were closely related to the play of power in the school. On the one hand, there was a faculty suspicious and resentful of outsiders, whom they saw as challenging their authority and usurping their prerogatives. They disapproved of what we were doing and had no understanding of why we were doing it. They objected to our presence in the classroom, questioned our classroom techniques, and deplored what they saw as our "permissive" approach to discipline.

On the other hand, there was an indecisive administration dedicated to a policy of avoiding conflict and ready to appease whatever group threatened to disturb the peace. With the principal of Kennedy Junior High, not a tight ship but a quiet one was the desired end. Under the circumstances, maintaining a quiet ship meant catering to his staff's objections. The spring before, setting up the Academy program had served a similar purpose in appeasing the fears of parents about school violence.

School and Sounding Board were, after all, involved in a marriage of convenience. In a certain sense it was a fair exchange. We were getting a chance to test the therapeutic classroom idea. The principal and his assistants were getting a device for controlling disruptive students, which, for the time being, would ease the immediate crisis of parent protest. Unfortunately, our goals were too far apart for the marriage to remain stable. The incompatibility went too deep. Our interests and priorities were light-years apart.

We were trying to build a model of education that could work effectively for low-achieving students. Our first priority was to meet their emotional and academic needs. The administration was trying to survive. Their first priority was the smooth operation of the school and the welfare of its teachers. They may have seemed ready to undertake an innovative experiment, but enthusiasm soon evaporated when the crisis was past. Never once did the principal take the time to sit down in the Academy and observe what was going on. It was not until June that his chief assistant principal sat through an Academy class, when we complained vehemently about his lack of interest.

Lack of interest in itself would not have been a serious problem for the Academy program. What did matter was the barrage of criticism and complaints that produced a continuing atmosphere of tension. It was like living in a stage of siege. Warding off attacks became a routine part of the Academy operation. Over and over it was necessary to explain our philosophy and objectives and to justify once more the most basic elements in the program.

Curriculum was an issue that never died. Settled definitively one week, it would emerge the next in a new form. What were the students learning? Why were they reading "cheap" literature? Why was there no precise plan for what would be covered during the next month? Or we would be presented with incongruous suggestions for subject matter. Teach respect for property by presenting the history of chairs and their uses. Give a lesson on the spinning wheel to develop an appreciation of the American Revolution.

However varied the complaints, they stemmed from the same roots: discomfort with our unorthodox ways and a failure to comprehend or accept the world and lifestyle of disadvantaged adolescents. Not surprisingly, the students' behavior and our approach to discipline came up for constant review. Why were our students out in the halls? Why did we permit them to chew gum? Why were they walking around in the classroom? Why were we taking no action when they used four-letter words? Why were they sitting on window sills and sprawled on the floor when they read by themselves?

In the value system of this administration, concern for propriety and bureaucratic rules took distinct precedence over other considerations. When Academy students made the breakthrough to reading books for the first time in their lives, the only reaction was a criticism of the way they were sitting. Arlene Friedman and Susan Jaffe spent long hours making up individual math sheets, the only reaction was to criticize the amount of paper being used. When ex-Academy students came back to visit the following fall, the only reaction was an anxious query as to whether they had passes.

178   Learning how to operate within an unsympathetic milieu

may have been the most valuable lesson of all. For a program like the therapeutic classroom to be viable, the problems it may encounter must be recognized for what they are. There is, after all, no future for the idea, if it can only function in a supportive context. There are not likely to be many of those around for quite a while. We may not have all the answers to the problems likely to arise in a traditional school, but we do have some. We are sure, for instance, that an all-out liaison effort is essential, more than we ourselves invested in during the Academy year. Most important, we know what can be expected and that, in one situation at least, the therapeutic classroom "worked," even in hostile territory.

References

Brenton, M. (1970), *What's Happened to Teacher?* New York: Avon Books.
Sarason, S. B. (1971), *The Culture of the School and the Problem of Change.* Boston: Allyn and Bacon.

CHAPTER 11

Toward a
Therapeutic Model—
A Realistic Proposal

I
F THE THERAPEUTIC CLASSROOM idea is only another beautiful dream to be filed away under "future possibilities," then we are wasting our time. Future panaceas are irrelevant for the millions of young people whose present learning deficits forecast a life of deprivation. What is needed, as is stated in Bard (1972), is to find "how change is possible not in terms of miracles but in basic reforms that are realistic in terms of our schools in our city" The therapeutic classroom approach offers such a model for reform in the "wasteland" of the intermediate schools, where hope has been abandoned for too many.

That's a big claim. Let us see what grounds there are for making it.

In the first place, apart from any considerations of humanitarianism, the precarious state of affairs in the urban high schools has forced the issue. There is unmistakable evidence all over the country that public alarm is, at last, opening the way for a serious rescue operation in the disaster area of secondary education. Remedial interest and material resources continue to favor the younger child and the early grades, but exploratory efforts to salvage adolescent learning casualties are on the increase. If nothing else, the mounting crisis of in-school violence, drug abuse, and mass truancy has put inaction out of the question.

Almost every big city is experimenting with one or more innovations aimed at controlling the epidemic of failure and its calamitous side effects. Since the latter tends to arouse the most apprehension, it is not surprising that the lion's share of attention is going to the senior high schools, where antisocial fallout from learning failure escalates. Innovations range from student-planned courses and paraprofessional programs to credit-for-work options and informal, satellite schools. In New York City close to twenty "mini" senior high schools have been organized as alternatives for students who cannot make it in the conventional monoliths.

The readiness of public school establishments to institute changes involving basic alterations in conventional procedures is a *sine qua non* for the realization of the therapeutic classroom model. What we are seeing now goes beyond readiness. It is fair to say that there is a widespread eagerness to find solutions for a problem that cannot be wished away. This is not to argue that a drastic educational revolution is going on. We can expect to find traditional approaches and modes of organization continuing. This is exactly what provides a realistic base for innovation.

If a revolution were necessary before change were possible, then the therapeutic classroom idea would indeed be a Utopian, never-never land proposal. The fact that the established system is showing enough flexibility to try fairly radical changes without a revolution makes the idea a here-and-now proposal. It is realistic as to what could be possible within the present public school context, given a continuing willingness to reassess priorities and techniques both by the school and the mental health clinics.

The realistic character of the therapeutic classroom model is further emphasized by its convergence with the experience and conclusions of others who have paid attention to low-achieving children past the elementary years. Whenever a genuine concern has been directed to young adolescent school failures, especially from minority and disadvantaged backgrounds, strikingly similar kinds of diagnoses and proposals have emerged. Threading through them like a leitmotif are a number of common themes: the school environment as the object of change, the role of personal relationships and reinforcement in dealing with the dynamics of failure, the development of skills and the capacity to function in society as primary teaching goals. The therapeutic classroom model shares these conclusions but takes them a giant step forward with its proposal of an indivisible bond between learning failure and emotional dynamics; this link precludes success by either pedagogy or therapy alone.

Directing remedial attention to the school environment does not mean that wider social factors are considered irrelevant for learning failure. Concerned educators are agreed, however, that outside environmental effects have served too long as convenient scapegoats for the failure that takes place in the schools. To say that these must change before the schools can succeed is as good as saying that the prospects for present adolescent learning casualties are hopeless. If disadvantaged and minority youngsters came from secure homes where they received the benefits of the "hidden curriculum" that equips the middle-class child for educational survival, there would be no problem in the first place or, at least, the problem would be different. The only hope lies in facing the situation as it exists without face-saving rationalizations or pretense.

The adolescent learning casualties of traditional education can be rescued if the school environment matches their needs. To do anything less is to bear the guilt for their defeated lives. The fact that they have failed does not mean that they are incapable of succeeding, as the schools have been insisting up to now. It does mean that they have been deprived of a learning environment that takes cognizance of their needs. Pointing to school responsibility for failure, Bloom (1972) writes: "There is growing evidence that much of what we termed individual differences in school learning is the effect of particular school conditions rather than of basic differences in the capabilities of students (p. 9).

The urgency of restructuring the school milieu in the post-elementary grades is emphasized, ironically enough, by the arguments offered by an advocate of reform for stressing the years from five to ten. Maintaining that faulty education is the main cause of school failure, Glasser (1969), urges that the major effort should be in the elementary school, although children can be helped at any school level. However, "After age ten it takes more than a good school experience and, unfortunately, shortly after age ten he is thrust into junior and senior high situations where he has much less chance for a corrective educational experience" (p. 226).

For the young adolescent, a corrective educational experience must hinge on the dynamics of his "failure identity," Glasser (1969). This is another basic proposition that the therapeutic classroom idea shares with other prescriptions for failure in the secondary schools. The unanimity on this point is nothing short of remarkable, whether in theoretical analyses, ongoing programs, or by classroom teachers who have worked with disadvantaged students. Many have arrived at it independently, as we did. The central role of psychological damage in adolescent learning failure seems inescapable when the problem is faced realistically.

From our front-line vantage point, it was evident that by the time a youngster reaches junior high school the blockage is too formidable and the sense of failure is too imbedded for learning to occur in the ordinary classroom context. Educational research offers ample support for this conclusion. In a review of research trends, Bloom (1972) points to the considerable evidence that repeated success in school over a number of years produces a positive self-image and high self-esteem, what amounts to a type of immunization against emotional illness. Conversely, a history of repeated failure or low marks appears to reduce ability to withstand stress and anxiety. We are now beginning to understand, he concludes, "how schools may actually infect children with emotional difficulties" (p. 9).

That the emotional component of learning failure prescribes the need for one-to-one relationships and large doses of positive reinforcement is consistently emphasized in remedial efforts aimed at the secondary level. In New York City's minischools, street workers, who are typically young black men and women, have been brought into the program to work in this area. Their assignment is to help students with personal problems that are interfering with school and involve them in a trust relationship with an adult.

A study of teachers who were successful with dropout students found that they strongly stressed the personal element. These teachers, Brenton (1970) reports, operated with an awareness of the anxieties, deep feelings of inadequacy, and entrenched defense mechanisms with which the dropouts faced academic tasks. They understood that the youngsters could not start to learn before they had gained some self-respect and a feeling of acceptance. They not only went out of their way to give the students recognition for good work, but deliberately capitalized on their strong points so that they could experience success (Brenton, 1970, p. 185).

In the same vein, Herndon, (1971) describing the informal reading approach that worked with his junior high school nonreaders, attributes its success to the building of trust. He says, "It works not by method but by virtue of the measure of trust between you and the student who is very likely someone who has learned in school to avoid trust and must learn through you to accept it, as you have to learn it through him" (p. 157).

In the giant secondary schools, which few American adolescents escape, class size is compounded, with assembly-line organization to make such a personal teacher–student trust relationship as likely as snow in July. Successful students find the impersonality of secondary education painful, as evidence from California to New York demonstrates, but are able to function in spite of it. For students infected with the failure sickness, the impersonality puts functioning out of the question. One way or another, every remedial effort directed at adolescents, as far as we have discovered, shares with the therapeutic classroom model a recognition of this fact and an attempt to deal with it.

What makes the therapeutic classroom model different is that it faces the psychological issue squarely as the central factor in secondary school failure and places it where it belongs in a remedial program for young adolescents—at the very center. The concrete elements of the model—including form, content, and procedures—are specifics indicated by the psychological dynamics of learning failure. While there has been widespread agreement on the need to take account of psychological needs, the therapeutic classroom, more than taking them into account, makes these needs its point of departure.

The convergence among reformers also extends to practical teaching objectives and to the long-range goals shaping them. Here again ours is no voice crying in the wilderness. A hard-nosed insistence on the priority of skills and the abandonment of meaningless curriculum materials seems to be universal in serious remedial proposals. Over and over stress is placed on acquiring the fundamental proficiency essential for nonmenial employment, advanced education, and self-respect. Herndon's comment that you have "to be able to read in America in order to be equal" makes the point well.

Unfortunately, although such a change is often urged, few educators act to throw out the curriculum in favor of reading. One very powerful reason for this is the United Federation of Teachers, which allows secondary school teachers to insist that they will teach the subject matter in which they are licensed, rather than the subject matter of greatest need.

In the literature on remedial programs are repeated references to "relevance" and to starting "where they are." To explore adolescent school failure seems to insure the conclusion reached by the Sounding Board staff about appropriate material and the assignment of learning tasks. Anything less than a match with the student's current ability level and frame of reference is a guarantee of frustration and further failure. In other words, if curriculum material is not relevant, forget it. Relevance, furthermore, is a two-faceted proposition. Any task requiring skills that the student lacks is irrelevant to him. Any subject matter that fails to provide some motivating connection with his real or fantasy world is irrelevant to him.

If these propositions seem transparently obvious in face of the problem, it should be pointed out that, in fact, they challenge some of the most entrenched practices and assumptions in the schools. To begin with, once the notion of student-relevant material for learning failure is accepted, much of the standard curriculum that presently organizes public education has to be discarded. And, for a number of reasons, the standard curriculum occupies a near-sacrosanct position. Administratively, it sets up a seemingly foolproof, systemwide pattern that can be monitored by uniform tests. In theory, it insures educationally sound teaching by spelling out the course of study and preselecting textbooks. It ensures subject teachers the opportunity to teach what interests them. But, most important, the standard curriculum embodies a philosophy and a set of assumptions that have long dominated traditional education.

According to this view, there is an identifiable body of knowledge that every properly educated person should know in order to be a worthwile member of society. The chief function of formal education, above all at the post-primary levels, is to impart this knowledge. Of course, in a dynamic world of expanding intellectual horizons, the nature of the knowledge changes. Latin and Greek, for instance, have lost their earlier significance; the sciences have become imperative. While curriculum requires continuing reevaluation, it is possible, as well as necessary, to specify what subject areas should be included and what content covered at succeeding stages of the schooling sequence. This curriculum is teacher-relevant.

A student-relevant curriculum operates on a very different set of assumptions and values. Subject matter and content become matters of secondary importance. The first order of business is the development of competence. Rather than defining the teacher as a person who transmits knowledge, he is redefined as a person who increases another human being's ability to deal with information and relate successfully to the world around him.

From this perspective, the criterion for selecting teaching material is the extent to which it motivates an active response. It is not a question of learning the material but learning from the material. For this purpose a television show like *Mod Squad* may be more useful than *Hamlet*. What difference does it make whether a student knows that *Hamlet* is a story about a prince in Denmark who struggles with doubts about avenging his father's death or that Linc on *Mod Squad* must decide whether or not to turn his friend in to the police? Both will involve teacher and student in the problem of how to resolve a moral question.

The issue is acquiring the resources for successful functioning. Glasser (1969), puts it this way: "The goals of education are to give people the mental tools to deal effectively with new situations, to place fewer restrictions on their lives caused by fear of difficult problems, and to enable people to deal with new situations and difficult problems rationally rather than emotionally" (p. 43).

Despite receptive educators and sound theory, the therapeutic classroom idea could amount to little more than an armchair solution if it proposed an all-or-nothing formula. What makes the model realistic in throughly practical terms is its flexibility. It offers a perspective and a set of guiding principles, rather than an exact blueprint. The theme that structures it, the interdependence of learning failure and psychological dynamics, can be played out in many variations. The Academy program, which demonstrates only one of them, indicated some of the possibilities, as well as some of the unresolved questions.

These questions point to the diversity available within the therapeutic classroom framework. The answers are open-ended and can be expected to vary from one situation to another. One question, for instance, concerns the scope of a program, which could run the gamut, from taking in an entire school or comprising a school within a school to, in its most minimal form, covering two periods back-to-back in the schedule of a single group. Other questions involve class organization. How much structure should there be and what kind? Depending on the makeup of the students, emphasis might center on continuing small groups, on *ad hoc* groups, or on individual activity. On the other hand, treating the class as a unit for part of the time might prove productive for youngsters who require a well-defined milieu.

If one question predominates, it is undoubtedly how to work out staff responsibilities. The heart of the therapeutic classroom operation is the presence of two people who between them meet the students' pressing emotional and academic needs. How shall their roles be defined, and how do they interact? Should one concentrate on the therapeutic side of things and the other on teaching? Is it necessary that the second person be a trained psychologist? Should a teacher working with this approach have special training? There are few clues to be found in the outcomes of other two-person classroom arrangements, which have involved team teaching, assistant teachers, and paraprofessionals. None of these arrangements are attempting to integrate two distinct professions. Furthermore, their objectives are quite different. Laudable as these are, the therapeutic classroom is after different fish and, in fact, takes a whole different view of fishing.

To describe the core components of the therapeutic classroom model is to picture a learning environment geared to immediate interpersonal relationships. The sole criterion for any element incorporated into this environment, whether structural or methodological, is what the adolescent school failure requires in order to experience success. In technical terms we are talking about milieu therapy for the youngster with failure-induced personality deficits, about altering his school world in a way that will enable him to develop the ego resources he has failed to acquire. In the context of the public junior high school, this calls for a

190

two-pronged maneuver: changes in class organization and the application of therapeutic principles in teaching.

The basic structural changes are aimed at eliminating the disorienting confusion and impersonality of the departmental system, and at producing a consistent environment where a few significant adults are able to establish direct relationships with the students. They are highly concrete and can be listed item by item.

1. *Small classes*—Numbers hold the key to relationships. Class size must be small enough so that students can be seen as individuals, rather than in terms of how they fit into a group organization. With two adults in the room, the maximum may be twenty.

2. *Long class periods*—Students with learning problems have variable attention spans and attending styles and need more time to become focused. Longer periods are a necessity, too, to allow for therapeutic intervention. In a traditional public school, the simplest arrangement is to double up the conventional forty-five-minute periods.

3. *A Second adult*—There seems no way to provide continuing personal support and attention to twenty students in terms of their academic and emotional needs without the presence of two adults.

On-the-spot application of therapeutic thinking in the classroom, which involves a new fusion of teaching with mental health techniques, is inherently a fluid process that cannot be pinned down precisely. Obviously, what happens will be keyed to what is going on. Unlike teaching by lesson plan, therapeutic teaching derives its agenda from the developing needs of real-life students. However, there are a number of underlying principles that serve as its point of departure and offer guidelines for classroom operations.

On the academic side, tasks should mesh with individual capacities and emotional dynamics. This requires a thoroughly elastic, organic curriculum. Teaching emphasis should be on competence and skills, rather than subject matter, especially the skill of reading. For the most part, students should work in small groups.

On the psychological side, mental health techniques directed toward behavior modification, rather than self-analysis, should be used extensively to unblock disabling defenses and strengthen ego resources. In this connection, the stress should be on positive reinforcement, open discussions, and the development of trust. Therapeutic intervention—in the classroom and outside of it—should be based on the analysis of individual dynamics.

In actual practice we have found that therapeutic teaching has meant engaging in a procedure that is analogous to a diagnosis and treatment operation. In the Academy program we became increasingly aware that what we were doing involved a general tactic that followed with an inevitable logic from our goals and philosophy. We applied this tactic more deliberately in the seventh-grade program that we conducted this year. Out of this experience has come a clearer picture of the directions staffing patterns might take.

The tactic starts with a diagnosis of the child, a determination of exactly where he is at emotionally and academically. This evaluation presupposes a period of observation and demands sufficient understanding of emotional dynamics and learning processes so that the relevant diagnostic questions are asked—not that there is a handy, all-purpose set of questions that can be applied like a computerized checklist. In each case, the specific questions that are relevant for forming a diagnosis will be indicated by the youngster's behavior. But the kinds of questions that are asked will come from psychology and learning theory. The next tactical step is the formation of a treatment plan and, after that, the all-important follow-through, during which

the treatment plan and diagnosis are continually re-examined and modified as the student grows and changes.

Viewed in the light of this operation, what is needed to conduct a therapeutic classroom is a staff that can make the diagnosis and carry out the treatment. This can be accomplished by having a therapeutically trained person working directly in the classroom with the teacher, as we did in the Academy.

There are many possible candidates for this role: graduate students in social work or psychology, teachers moving up into guidance positions.

The therapeutic classroom points to the emergence of an entirely new professional category, the teacher–therapist. In the therapeutic classroom the role of the mental health person is not classically therapeutic, and the teacher is not enacting the classic teaching role. What happens is that the two become fused. We saw this taking place in the Academy without planning or premeditation. It is a development that seems to be a built-in feature of a realistic attempt to deal with learning failure in the postelementary years.

The therapeutic classroom model might well prevent teachers, as well as students, from dropping out. For many teachers it offers a setting where they can relate to students as they have wanted to but have found impossible under conventional conditions. Every year the schools lose large numbers of trained and motivated teachers who cannot tolerate the frustrations and constraints of assembly-line education.

Sarason (1971), discusses the dilemma of young teachers in a recent book. They are, he says "an eager, anxious, malleable group searching rather desperately for some kind of acceptable compromise between the realities of the classroom and their fantasies about being able to help children" (p. 171).

It is not only teachers but therapists as well who will have to be reoriented, if the needs of these adolescents are to be met. The cycle begins with the referral of an acting-out student to the guidance counselor, who refers him to the local mental health clinic. Here he almost never gets any help. At some historical point one of these professional groups will have to break out of the cycle and stop pretending. There are countless mental health professionals who would do better to spend their time in the classroom than in the clinic. Two entrenched systems have to change before this can happen: Schools have to overcome their sense of threat in the face of the dreaded outsider and mental health centers have to overcome the stultifying adherence to professionalism that prevents them from meeting community needs.

Hopefully, the recent emphasis in psychology on community programs will move the therapists away from office-based treatment to school-based consultation and interaction. The following discussion by Hersch (1972), points up the direction of the new emphasis within psychology:

> The conservative viewpoint sees the problem as residing in the individual and tries to change him; the reform viewpoint sees the problem as residing in the environment and tries to change it. A conservative viewpoint sees a troubled environment and blames it on individuals, a reform viewpoint sees troubled individuals and blames that on the environment.
>
> . . . what is at the core of the community mental health movement is a shift in the underlying professional ideology from a clinical to a public health frame of reference. . . .
>
> In the clinical orientation, the individual patient is identified and becomes the object of concern. He is a deviant from some norm of health, and this deviation is considered abnormal. The abnormality has the character of a disease and is regarded as a part of, or inside of, the person. It is a particular type of disease that is shared by some other people, and it can therefore be named and classified. The clinical aim of intervention is to change this person so that his condition is gone or so that its consequences are minimized. . . .

Now let us turn to the *public health* frame of reference. Here there is a move from a focus on the individual patient to a focus on large populations. The purpose of intervention is to reduce the incidence of disability or disease in such a population. Therefore, a special value is placed on primary prevention rather than on cure, and prevention paradigms are presented along with treatment paradigms. Professional attention is placed not only on the casualties of damaging environments but on the damaging environments themselves. . . (p. 750).

What we are proposing to mental health workers then, is a movement away from the clinical emphasis on the sickness of individuals to a public health emphasis on the school as a damaging environment. The whole Sounding Board program can be seen as an effort to modify that environment to meet the needs of individuals.

It may take a long time, but perhaps it is not too much to hope that the time will come when therapists who want to work with disadvantaged adolescents will spend their professional lives in the classroom, where they will be warmly welcomed by teachers and school administrators. Together, they can make a difference. We know that this is so, because we have seen it happen.

References

Bard B. (1972), Schools get failing grade. *New York Post*, January 14.

Bloom, B.S. (1972), *Report on Preschool Education*, August 9, 1972. Chicago: University of Chicago.

Brenton, M. (1970), *What's Happened to Teacher?* New York: Avon Books.

Glasser, W. (1969), *Schools without Failure*. New York: Harper & Row.

Herndon, J. (1971), *How to Survive in Your Native Land*. New York: Simon and Schuster.

Hersch, C. (1972), Social history, mental health, and community control. *American Psychologist*, 27 (8):749–754.

Sarason, S. B. (1971), *The Culture of the School and the Problem of Change*. Boston: Allyn and Bacon.

Index